THE REVOLUTIONARY WAR

THE REVOLUTIONARY WAR

DOUGLAS WELSH

Galahad Books · New York City

A Bison Book

First Published in the US by
Galahad Books
a division of A & W Publishers, Inc.
95 Madison Avenue
New York
New York 10016

Copyright © 1982 Bison Books Limited

Produced by
Bison Books Limited
4 Cromwell Place
London SW7

Library of Congress Catalog Card Number
81-86649

ISBN 0-88365-599-3

Printed in Hong Kong

CONTENTS

1 THE SEEDS OF REVOLUTION

Of all the American wars the Revolutionary War is perhaps most shrouded in patriotism, emotion and misinformation. This holds true for all wars from which new nations are born because credence must be given to the cause for which they are fought. Yet how did thirteen colonies, which normally had difficulty cooperating, unite into a common front against one of the greatest nations of the time? An American perspective gives just causes for the division. Tyranny, taxation without representation, repressive legislation and restrictive proclamations are all part of that perspective, and the Revolutionary leaders are revered as men of great vision and determination.

Despite this picture it is a misconception to believe that the years prior to the Revolution were years of discontent for the majority of colonists. It was in fact a European confrontation in the Americas, the Seven Years War or the French and Indian War as it is also known, that laid the foundation for the Revolution. The French and Indian War ended in 1763 and had two primary results for the colonies. After that war the colonies were secure from invasion from Canada, which was now under British rule. With the borders secure the colonists discovered that the war had brought not only security but prosperity. The British armies sent to fight on behalf of the colonies had to obtain supplies and provisions from the colonists. Equally naturally the Crown did not confiscate what it needed but bought supplies at a 'fair' price, though this was usually inflated by the colonists. Thus the

Below left: The British flag is raised at Fort Duquesne after its capture from the French in 1758 during the French and Indian War. George Washington, who took part in the campaign as an officer of the colonial militia, is seen raising his hat in salute in the center of the picture.

Above: A meeting between the Indian chief Pontiac and Robert Rogers, a Scotch-Irishman from New Hampshire, who led an irregular force of frontiersmen and scouts in the French and Indian War with great success. The tactics developed by such forces were used against the British and their allies throughout the War of Independence.

prosperity gained during the French and Indian War would launch many colonial merchants on a path of success which in time would lead to a clash with Britain.

It must also be recognized that until the pre-revolutionary years the colonies had not suffered the same tax burden as the native British. Of every 100 British subjects 20 resided in the colonies. Nineteen of that 20 were in some way involved in agriculture. Many farmers held large, well ordered, prosperous farms. The land owners of Virginia, Maryland and the Carolinas held plantations which were showing enormous profits. The other individual of the 20 was likely to be involved in trade or in manufacturing businesses, such as metal or glass making or mining. American silversmiths were some of the best in the world. Their conservative designs gave their work an austere beauty which has survived to the present as examples of functional artwork. In woodwork American craftsmen led their field. Even with only 20 percent of the British population the American colonies were without a doubt highly productive.

In such a situation it is small wonder that Parliament began to recognize the colonies as a source of income because they had for too long enjoyed the full benefits of British protection without paying a fair share of the costs. Following closely behind the French and Indian War came the Pontiac Indian Uprising of 1763. Once again the British Army was sent to quell the threat. To help with the maintenance of the additional 7000 troops needed Parliament approached the colonies with a nex tax. The Stamp Duty was ordered as a seal to be used on all legal documents, newspapers, licenses and other official documents which would raise approximately one half of the expense incurred for the defense of the colonies against Pontiac and to help maintain a future defense budget. Parliament allowed the colonies one year to decide if this was the proper means to collect the necessary revenue and gave the colonists the right through the colonial Governors to suggest more equitable and acceptable methods. This Parliamentary license was somewhat unprecedented and did give the colonies a voice in their taxation system. The point which is most often overlooked in considering the Stamp Act is that the funds raised through it would be used directly to benefit the Colonies. Parliament's willingness to compromise on an alternative system would be the first of many gestures which gave the lie to the claim of taxation without representation. The fact remained that finance had to be found for upkeep of the British Army in the Americas, regardless of the means employed.

When peace came after the Pontiac Uprising it brought with it one of the major causes for initial hostility between the colonies and Britain. In October 1763 a royal proclamation declared the Appalachian Mountain region to be the western-most boundary of the colonies. Land west of the Appalachians was forbidden for colonization as land belonging to the Indians. To the British who wrote the treaty ending the uprising this seemed fair. The colonists did not have an over-population problem nor did Britain foresee any need for the enlargement of the colonies. The British were weary of war in America and the burdens war created and this agreement was considered reasonable to attain peace. However, the colonists, or at least a selected portion of them, found the proclamation inhibiting. The fur traders and land speculators saw the enormous region west of the Appalachians as a vast untapped resource. Many of the colonies had already laid claim to this region as a means of expanding their borders and for a few it meant an unlimited source of wealth.

The colonists failed to devise an alternative to the Stamp Act and it eventually came into effect in 1765. A further source of trouble was the passage of the Currency Act in 1764 prohibiting the American colonies from issuing their own currency. It was in this year also that the colonists began to feel the pressure of Parliament's taxes. Not only were new taxes being levied but the British government was becoming more demanding in the collection of those taxes. The colonists continued to pay far less in tax than their counterparts in Britain but there were those who saw the levying and execution of the tax collections as interference in colonial affairs. The colonies had been for so long relatively ignored by England because of the greater attractions of India and the West Indies that the institution of control by Parliament was felt as a challenge to the freedom that had been enjoyed.

It is important to note that the majority of weight being laid on the colonies by these taxes was not placed on the common man but on business concerns, on the wealthy merchant and agricultural controlling class. This is not to say that the Stamp Act did not affect the common man, but it did not encroach on his life in any significant way. Here is the foundation of the initial revolution movement. The merchant class saw its enormous profits being slowly eroded by English taxes and the land speculators saw their horizons being limited.

Parliament continued in a conciliatory manner with regard to the taxation issues and many collection agents in the colonies were grateful for the recognition given to the peculiar situation. The British Prime Minister George Grenville made it clear to the colonists that England's responsibility for the maintenance of peace and prosperity in the Empire could not be met without the support of the colonies in paying their fair share of that expense. But the colonists refused to acknowledge this fact. When the Stamp Act was finally imposed the merchants of Boston, Massachusetts flew flags at half-mast and church bells were muffled as they were for funerals. Speeches were made against the Act and newspaper

articles denounced the tax. Patrick Henry, a Virginia lawyer who became prominent during this controversy, condemned Parliament saying that the taxation of the colonies should be done by the colonial governments. Approval was given by the Virginia Assembly for this policy though they realized that they had little authority to carry it out.

The hostility was growing and the seeds of revolution were being planted in those who had the most to lose by an increase in Parliamentary control over the colonies. Although for this early time they were extremists a fellowship known as the Sons of Liberty was formed which challenged the Stamp Act whenever possible. The leader of this group was a politician and activist from New England, Samuel Adams, who not only argued for the repeal of the Act but for an examination of the entire relationship between the colonies and England. Stamp-masters' houses were ransacked in Boston. In Williamsburg, Virginia, mobs gathered outside the Stamp-master's home threatening him while in Maryland a mob destroyed the Stamp-master's store. Throughout the colonies agents of the Crown were attacked or their homes and businesses destroyed in retaliation for Parliament's proclamation. However, this retaliation was not as spontaneous as many were led to believe. Much of the reaction was a result of well organized assaults by Adams' Sons of Libery.

By October 1765 Adams and his followers had whipped up such opposition to the Stamp Act that a delegation of all the Colonies met in New York. At this 'Congress' it was agreed that they would petition Parliament to revoke the Act. To give strength to their petition the 'Congress' called on all colonists to boycott British goods. Once again this surge of patriotism is somewhat tarnished when put into total perspective. The delegates to this Congress were men of rank; lawyers, merchants and businessmen. In calling for the boycott of British goods they would not only demonstrate unity within the colonies but would create a demand for goods produced in the colonies. The purchase of those goods, which were generally more expensive than their British counterparts, would bring even greater profits for colonial merchants in a closed market place. But the colonists were just beginning to consider themselves as something other than Englishmen and they rallied to the boycott issue. Cancellation of orders for British goods began immediately and British merchants became alarmed. When Parliament received the petition it immediately debated the issue. After long and often bitter discussions the Stamp Act was repealed by a narrow margin.

Parliament had been split by the Stamp Act question but not to such a degree that it could not agree that something had to be done to demonstrate Britain's control over the colonies. That demonstration was made in the Declaratory Act of 1766. This act had little impact in the colonies initially as they were occupied with celebrations of the defeat of the Stamp Act. The Declaratory Act basically stated that Parliament had full power and authority to make laws which were binding on the peoples and colonies of the Americas in all cases. While others rejoiced Samuel Adams realized the ramifications of the Declaratory Act and raised serious questions about the right of the British Parliament to make laws binding on the colonies. The representation issue was brought abruptly to the forefront. As the colonies had no Members of Parliament could they expect just treatment from Parliament? This ignored the fact that Parliament had recently shown by its openness to petition that it was not oblivious to the concerns and wishes of the colonies.

There was, however, a subtle shift in parliamentary opinion with the Americans losing several of their sympathetic friends, such as William Pitt who stepped down owing to failing health and was replaced by his chancellor Charles Townshend. Townshend, like most of his Parliamentary collegues, realized that the colonists disliked direct taxation and began to devise indirect methods for the raising of revenues. Townshend also advocated a less tolerant stand by Parliament, which would give ammunition to activists in the colonies. The Revenue Act of 1767 was imposed

Above: Samuel Adams (1722–1803) after a painting by John Copley.
Below: A confrontation between British troops and colonists.

The·TIMES are Dreadful, Dismal Doleful Dolorous, and DOLLAR-LESS.

Thursday, October 31, 1765.   THE   NUMB. 1195.

PENNSYLVANIA JOURNAL;
AND
WEEKLY ADVERTISER.

EXPIRING: In Hopes of a Resurrection to LIFE again.

I AM sorry to be obliged to acquaint my Readers, that as The STAMP-ACT, is fear'd to be obligatory upon us after the First of November ensuing, (the fatal To-morrow) the Publisher of this Paper unable to bear the Burthen, has thought it expedient to stop a while, in order to deliberate, whether any Methods can be found to elude the Chains forged for us, and escape the insupportable Slavery, which it is hoped, from the last Representations now made against that Act, may be effected. Mean while, I must earnestly Request every Individual of my Subscribers. many of whom have been long behind Hand, that they would immediately Discharge their respective Arrers that I may be able, not only to support myself during the Interval, but be better prepared to proceed again with this Paper, whenever an opening for that Purpose appears, which I hope will be soon
WILLIAM BRADFORD

Left: An example of contemporary propaganda aimed against the Stamp Act. The radical colonists produced a great many very effective pamphlets and engravings to support their case.
Right: A demonstration against the Stamp Act in Boston.

to replace the Stamp Act. The Townshend Act levied import duties on common articles like glass, paper, lead and even paint pigments. The tax would lead to higher prices in the colonies as merchants sought to recoup their importation losses but such duties were perfectly normal. Had Parliament halted there the outcry would probably not have been overwhelming. The colonists might have grumbled but they could not justifiably claim that they were being subjected to an unusual punishment. However, Parliament added a provision to enforce the Act, legalizing a Writ of Assistance. This was actually a search warrant provision to assist government officials in their role as agents of the Crown. Such writs permitted officials to search ships, businesses and homes to find articles on which the proper import taxes had not been paid. This could be determined by the presence of a tax seal on legal items. Originally Parliament considered this as a means to halt the massive smuggling operations being conducted in the colonies. Under British law such writs could only be used when the agent had just cause and evidence to warrant a search. However, a great deal of pressure was being placed on agents to stop the smuggling and customs officials carried with them a general writ that permitted them to search at will with only the official's zealous suspicions as cause. Warrants for such searches had been in occasional use for some time and those colonial merchants who were primarily involved in the smuggling operations, such as John Hancock, had opposed the writs as illegal and an 'invasion of the rights of every Englishman.' The merchants had taken their case to court, represented by John Otis who in his remarks denounced the writs as an 'open door for any man prompted by revenge, greed or

ill-humor' to enter another man's home or business for no good reason. When with the Townshend Act Parliament legalized full use of the writs, anger swept through the colonies. Many asked how Parliament could impose such an act on citizens of the Crown. Others showed their disgust by refusing to provide quarters for British soldiers. In New York such action was taken and Parliament responded by revoking the New York 'right to (have an) Assembly.' Circulars appeared calling for the repeal of Parliament's acts. Samuel Adams again rose to the foreground as he promoted dissent and appealed for yet another embargo on British goods. He also suggested that colonists should refuse to buy clothing made in England and begin to wear the 'homespun' of the colonies to display their contempt.

As a result of the action taken against the New York Assembly other legislative bodies began to listen more closely to men like Adams. Georgia, South Carolina, Maryland and Massachusetts supported Adams' stance and New York's plight, calling for unity among all colonies against Parliament's actions. Their rights to assembly were also revoked and their legislators strictly forbidden to meet. The Virginia House of Burgesses adopted a set of resolutions which they believed summarized the colonies' position appealing to Parliament not only for the repeal of the Townshend Act but for the reinstatement of the assemblies of the effected colonies. Finally they asked Parliament to give colonial legislators the right to levy taxes on the colonies rather than have this done by direct proclamation from London. Had Parliament objectively considered this proposal further confrontation might have been avoided. The assemblies could have called for taxes in their own name, giving a false sense of

self-determination while at the same time passing the revenues on to those areas for which Parliament was actually raising funds. However, both Parliament and the colonies had reached a point of belligerence. Parliament considered the colonists, particularly certain of their leaders, as nothing more than troublesome rabble unwilling to meet their responsibility to King and Country. The colonies were beginning to view Britain as an oppressive meddler rather than the 'Mother Country.'

By 1768 the situation was more strained. In the colonies British soldiers were being harassed and taunted, subjected to both verbal and physical abuse. Troops standing guard or marching from post to barracks were pelted with rocks and in winter with snowballs. The British forces responded with disciplined restraint by refusing to retaliate to such treatment. In fact the majority of soldiers considered the harassment the work of irresponsible, isolated undesirables not as a reflection of the colonists as a whole. As the climate became more hostile members of the Board of Customs Commission grew concerned about their personal safety and requested increased military assistance, complaining that the garrison regiments throughout the colonies could not react quickly enough to counter an outbreak of violence. It was agreed in Parliament that a show of force, particularly in Boston, might be advantageous. The

warship HMS *Romney* sailed to Boston with orders to aid in the routing of smugglers and with letters restating the obligation of the British command in that city to the Board of Customs officials.

On 10 June 1768, shortly after the *Romney* arrived the sloop *Liberty* was seized with a cargo of contraband goods en route to Boston. The tension was heightened by the fact that the vessel's log indicated it belonged to John Hancock, who was not only one of the wealthiest merchants in the town but a close friend of Samuel Adams. As an example to others the *Liberty* was towed into Boston harbor and put under the guns of HMS *Romney*. The result of this was a violent riot in Boston, which Adams and Hancock helped to incite. During the violence Board Commissioners were attacked and their homes vandalized. Several of the British boats used to collect duty in the harbor were burned in view of Hancock's home. The situation became so grim that four Commissioners were forced to flee for their lives to the *Romney* then seek the protection of the fort in Boston Harbor. The people of Boston held a town meeting to call for the removal of the *Romney*, claiming that its presence was antagonizing an already volatile situation as a symbol of aggressive policies toward all Bostonians.

The violence produced relatively swift action as the Commissioners demanded more military aid. Two additional regiments arrived and several more warships were dispatched to support the *Romney*. This information, given to Samuel Adams by an informant, was announced at the town meeting. The people were roused to anger and Adams gave full vent to his rhetorical prowess by warning them to keep their weapons by their sides 'like fine Englishmen should' in the event the 'French' chose to attack. John Otis had reminded Adams not to advocate armed rebellion against Britain's representatives as it would give the authorities cause to invoke the Mutiny Act of 1766 against those present at the meeting. Otis' calm logic contained Adams and kept armed conflict from erupting at this point. For all Adams' urging the general mood in Boston was not yet ripe for open rebellion. The majority wanted simply to return to the conditions prior to 1764, believing that trouble-makers on both sides of the Atlantic were the source of most of the problems. In the merchant class, particularly for those not involved in smuggling operations, the most sought after goal was a return to business as usual. Adams' attempts to promote open defiance were relatively unsuccessful as the four British regiments in the Boston area had a sobering effect on the community.

Within the year the situation though uneasy had calmed to such an extent that two of the British regiments were withdrawn to Halifax. Confrontations had been reduced to the occasional stone thrown or brawls in local taverns. However, Adams was not prepared to let the issues fade into oblivion. He began publishing the 'Journal of the Times.' This circular was devoted entirely to anti-British propaganda. Its articles were concerned with daily incidents between colonists and British troops. Stories of rape, robbery and senseless violence perpetrated by British soldiers filled its pages. In time the people of Boston began to believe that all the stories were fact; they usually 'occurred' elsewhere in the colonies. In later years John Otis would admit that the majority of articles were fabricated, some 90 percent having no foundation in truth. Throughout 1769 tension continued to mount. Otis himself was attacked in a coffee house for remarks he made and beaten severely enough that he had to be carried to his home. The incident gave Adams more fuel for his fire. In November Adams retaliated for that beating by having several customs informers tarred and feathered.

The same pattern of events continued at the beginning of 1770 but in February an incident occurred which irrevocably united many Bostonians against the British. Adams and members of the Sons of Liberty rallied a mob outside the home of a customs informer threatening to burn his house down around him. The man, fearing for his life, fired into the crowd killing an 11 year old boy. British troops arrived and immediately put the agent under arrest for murder. In the trial which followed the man was found guilty and sentenced to jail. Adams led the public outcry

stating that British sympathizers could kill children and not pay the full penalty for it. In fact many in Boston and other colonies had no knowledge of the extenuating circumstances nor was it made widely known that the man did indeed receive a prison sentence. The hostile mood in Boston increased and on 5 March 1770 another crowed gathered outside the Customs House. The lone sentry called for assistance when the crowd began pelting him with rocks and threatening his life. A detachment of the 29th Regiment under the command of Captain Thomas Preston went to the sentry's aid. Preston ordered the mob to disperse but they refused, hurling stones and snowballs at the troops. Witnesses later testified that Preston screamed more loudly at his own men to maintain discipline than he did at the crowd. In the confusion the word 'fire' was heard and the tense soldiers volleyed into the crowd. Three citizens died immediately and another two were mortally wounded. Adams now had an explosive incident which he would use to the best advantage in generating open hostility against England. The British command in Boston jailed Preston and his men. Adams demanded that the men be tried for murder. To his surprise his own brother John Adams and associates defended the troops. Witnesses testified that the troops had been attacked by a mob and that no one could positively say from where the order to fire originated. Preston and all but two of the soldiers were acquitted. Those two were held for court-martial, branded and dismissed

Above: The Boston Massacre. British troops fire on the crowd. As the small caption at the bottom states the original of this illustration was 'Engrav'd Printed & Sold by Paul Revere *Boston*' better known for the ride from Lexington to Concord.
Left: The death of the boy Snider which provoked the riot leading to the Boston Massacre.
Below right: How a tea ship was prevented from landing its cargo.

from the service. Throughout that time Samuel Adams exploited the incident in his 'Journal' calling it 'The Boston Massacre.' One of those killed was a former slave, Crispus Attucks, whom Adams used to illustrate that it was the duty of every colonist to fight for freedom as had the man who had known slavery.

In England the new Prime Minister Lord North urged the repeal of the Townshend Act. Parliament also allowed the Quartering Act of 1765 to expire. Although these acts were set aside Parliament reaffirmed its contention that the colonies were still under British rule and that some tax must be levied for the maintenance of colonial defense, taking the situation back to its origin. With the Townshend Act repealed the less radical viewpoint prevailed in spite of Samual Adams' attempts to promote dissent. It was widely accepted that senseless bloodshed would accomplish little and a new cooperation was sought by both sides.

For the next two years the colonists and the British government attempted to find a means by which both could accomplish their goals without creating further rifts between them. However, in June 1772 the situation flared once again. The British revenue ship HMS *Gaspée* was attacked and burned by radical colonists. The colonists claimed that they were merely protecting themselves from an attack by the vessel. In fact the vessel had virtually brought smuggling in the Rhode Island area to a halt and wealthy New England merchants took advantage of the vessel's

running aground in pursuit of a smuggler and destroyed it. Although the British crew was saved the captain of the *Gaspée* was shot. The British authorities stated that the guilty parties would be sent to Britain for trial. The situation was made worse when the colonial authorities in Rhode Island made little effort to capture the perpetrators. Rhode Island had been self-governing but this status was changed when the Crown announced that in future it would pay the salaries of the governor and judges rather than allow the Colonial Assemblies to do so. In this way the British hoped to overcome conflicts of interest.

These measures brought Samuel Adams to prominence once again, leading Boston's citizens and establishing a 'Committee of Correspondents' whose task was to keep the colonies informed and to take the 'truth' to the rest of the civilized world. In Massachusetts John Otis was made chairman of the 21 member committee. Other prominent colonial leaders served on similar committees in their own regions. Patrick Henry and Thomas Jefferson were key members in Virginia. As there was no unified Colonial Assembly this organization would provide the loose structure of one to organize the colonies if the situation should worsen.

One issue which was becoming increasingly important but which was less widely publicized was the proclamation against the expansion of the colonies beyond the Appalachian Mountains. Wealthy colonists like George Washington, remembered for his surveying of the area, had invested large sums of money in land there. Now, 10 years later they saw little hope of

To the Public.

THE long expected TEA SHIP arrived last night at Sandy-Hook, but the pilot would not bring up the Captain till the sense of the city was known. The committee were immediately informed of her arrival, and that the Captain solicits for liberty to come up to provide necessaries for his return. The ship to remain at Sandy-Hook. The committee conceiving it to be the sense of the city that he should have such liberty, signified it to the Gentleman who is to supply him with provisions, and other necessaries. Advice of this was immediately dispatched to the Captain; and whenever he comes up, care will be taken that he does not enter at the custom-house, and that no time be lost in dispatching him.
New-York, April 19, 1774.

recovering their investments unless Britain revoked that proclamation or the colonies split from the Empire.

By 1773 the British East India Company was suffering from the boycotts imposed by colonial buyers. When the Townshend Act was repealed Parliament had placed a duty on tea and New England merchants smuggled Dutch tea rather than pay that duty. Tea had been chosen by Parliament as it was a commodity used by all which would ensure even distribution of the tax to all colonists. It was believed that as each colonist would only be required to pay a small percentage of the duty that a fair and equitable taxing method had been found. Parliament was wrong. The colonists considered the tax on their tea yet another case of Britain arbitrarily asserting its power to tax the colonies. Faced with the drop in sales Parliament first granted the East India Company large public loans then worked out a system whereby the company could sell its tea at a cheaper price. Initially all tea from the East India Company had to pass through London where the taxes were assessed before merchants purchased and shipped the tea to such points as the American colonies. This was changed to allow the East India Company to ship its tea directly to the colonies from its source. The resulting lower prices would offset the tax being levied resulting in lower prices for tea than ever before. The lower price should appease the colonists and at the same time force the smugglers, whose tea was very expensive by comparison, out of operation. The plan was logical and efficient. However, the colonists, particularly the New England merchants and Samuel Adams, found fault with the scheme. Adams claimed that 'cheap tea was a cheap trick' to herald more taxes on other sought-after items in the future. The merchants saw the cheap tea as an end to their lucrative smuggling operations as well as a means of cutting their shipping revenues when the East India Company began shipping direct. Not only that but Parliament had given approval to the East India Company to chose its merchants in the colonies. Obviously men like Hancock who were known to be rabble-rousers and suspected smugglers were not given such merchant licenses. Thus Parliament and the East India Company were accused of creating a tea monopoly, a development to which the majority of merchants in the colonies were adamantly opposed.

Adams used this issue to provoke a demonstration. He knew that once the colonists realized the savings to be made by buying the less expensive tea his credibility would suffer. When the tea arrived in Boston harbor Adams began his agitation. The situation became so volatile that the ship-masters

decided not to risk an incident and prepared to leave the port. However, the governor claimed that the ships owed duty for entering the harbor and would not permit them to leave until it was paid. The shippers therefore decided that it would be best to sell the cargo, pay the duty and leave with some profit rather than lose everything. Twenty days were granted in which they could pay the toll. On 17 December during a town meeting Adams gave a rousing speech. In answer to his questions of what should be done a group of colonists arrived dressed as Mohawk Indians. Rallying support from all in the hall they rushed off to the harbor. Altogether 340 chests of tea were dumped into the water and several vessels were burned. To keep the British from retaliating the mob brought with it women and children, knowing that they would not be fired on. The incident would soon become known as the 'Boston Tea Party.' Adams' example was followed elsewhere and although many in the colonies approved others were shocked at such violence. For Parliament it was the last in a series of incidents which could no longer be tolerated.

Parliament believed it had been lenient. The primary issue had been to find a means by which the colonies could pay a minimum of their own defense expense, which Parliament continued to view as a reasonable request. The refusal to pay specific taxes was one matter but the increased violence and destruction of property was quite another. Parliament overwhelmingly passed four measures to stabilize the situation. These measures would become known throughout the colonies as the 'Intolerable Acts' of 1774. The first act was to close Boston Harbor until the colonists paid for all loss and damage incurred. The second was to cancel the Massachusetts Charter and forbid town meetings in the colony. The third was a new Quartering Act which stated that colonists would have to provide food and lodging for all troops sent to keep law and order. Finally, any British officer accused of a crime in the execution of his duty to uphold the law would be returned to Britain for trial. Also passed was the Quebec Act of 1774 which extended the boundaries of Quebec, enlarging the province to encompass all territory south to the Ohio River and west to the Mississippi. This immediately enraged the land speculators. This act also permitted the French population in Quebec to practice their Catholic religion. Although this had no real relevance to the colonists, men like Adams claimed that the British government was legitimizing Catholicism and asked if the British might not next allow an Inquisition in the colonies.

The New England colonists had no intention of submitting to the Intolerable Acts. British authority was openly defied. The British commander in the colonies, General Thomas Gage, was established as Governor of Massachusetts and given more troops to maintain order. Massachusetts was being used as an example to other radicals in the colonies. The extent of the British reaction startled other assemblies and spread resentment and fear throughout the colonies. On 5 September delegates sent from all the colonies except Georgia met in what would become known as the First Continental Congress. At the meeting several resolutions were adopted. King George III had stated that the colonists must decide whether they wished to remain loyal to the Crown or become independent of it. The independence issue was strongly denied and although the Congress gave assurances that they wished to remain English they made certain demands on Parliament. The delegates issued a request for the reinstitution of the Massachusetts Charter and called upon Parliament to recognize their rights and to respect those rights as they would those of a British citizen living in Britain. They also requested the exclusive right to legislate in the colonies in business and legal affairs. The Congress advocated a return to the boycott of British goods and advised the colonies to create their own local committees for 'safety and inspection' to show a solid front against future Parliamentary action. Finally the delegates agreed to meet again in the spring of 1775 to discuss further action in the event Parliament chose to ignore their demands.

In many parts of the colonies organizations known as the Minutemen took shape; militia who were to be prepared to respond 'on a minute's notice' to the call to arms. These units began to hoard supplies and ammunition. Samuel Adams and John Hancock,

under orders of arrest for treason against the Crown, went into hiding near Lexington, Massachusetts where there was a strong radical element and where arms and supplies were being stored. The wheels of rebellion had been set in motion. Records show that General Gage received information from an agent that Lexington and Concord were rallying points for the colonial activists and that weapons were being stored there in large quantities. There is evidence that Adams himself had a hand in leaking this information in an effort to force a confrontation. Gage had to respond but he did not want to instigate open conflict. The Bostonian radicals, expecting a reaction, agreed upon a system to warn of any British activity. On the night of 18 April 1775 a small band of 'Patriots' in Charlestown saw the signal given from the old North Church in Boston. The signal told them by which route the British were advancing in their bid to eliminate the supplies at Lexington and Concord. The warning was carried by three riders. Paul Revere has become the most noted of the messengers but he was actually captured before he traveled the full distance. However, William Dawes and Dr Samuel Prescott managed to ride all the way to Concord.

The British troops crossed the Charles River and marched along the road to Concord. By dawn on 19 April they had reached Lexington where a small group of Minutemen had assembled on the village green under the command of their militia captain John Parker. Major Pitcairn, commanding the British troops, ordered the colonists to lay down their arms

Above: After the fight at Lexington the return march of the British to Boston turned into a running battle. Here colonists are shown firing on the retreating British.
Left: Paul Revere's famous ride on the night of 18 April 1775 as seen in a nineteenth century illustration.

promising that if they did so the incident would be considered closed and they might return to their homes peacefully. John Parker with only 77 men realized that his situation was hopeless. He had earlier told his men not to fire unless fired upon but to stand their ground. His words, 'but if they mean to have war let it begin here' would become prophetic. His position was untenable, however, and to avoid senseless bloodshed he ordered his men to move away from the green but not to lay down their arms. At that tense moment a shot rang out. No one has ever been able to say positively from where. The British troops responded immediately with several volleys and when the smoke had cleared eight colonists were dead and 10 more wounded. The Minutemen quickly dispersed. Upon hearing the

gunfire Adams allegedly announced that it was 'the start of a glorious morning.' The course he had apparently been trying to set was being taken.

Pitcairn's force moved on to Concord where they cut down the Liberty Pole and set fire to the courthouse. The only supplies they could find were a few artillery carriages left behind when the colonists hastily removed their cache of equipment. As Pitcairn organized his men for the return to Boston he discovered that a force of colonists had established a position near North Bridge. Colonel Barrett, their commander, had formed his men on Punkatasset Hill, a low ridge some 900 yards from the northern edge of the bridge. The position offered excellent protection for the militia from which to harass the British troops as they made their way back to Boston. By this time the countryside was swarming with militiamen who had heard of the events at Lexington. From every point of concealment they maintained a steady fire against the British troops, withdrawing whenever Pitcairn's men attempted to rout out their assailants. In early evening the British reached the

Three phases in the action on 19 April. Left: Some of the colonists on Lexington Green are hit as the redcoats fire a volley.
Right: A detail from the painting 'At Concord Bridge' by N C Wyeth.
Below: The retreating British column comes under fire from bands of colonists.

'safety' of Boston. The return march had cost 73 killed, 174 wounded and 26 unaccounted for of an original column of approximately 600 men. Although a relief force had gone to their aid the casualty rate was enormous when the actual accomplishments of the mission were considered.

Armed rebellion had begun. Before the night of 19 April was ended some 16,000 Minutemen surrounded Boston in answer to the call to arms. Colonists rallied to defend and support the liberties that they believed the Intolerable Acts were denying them but the revolution they began was founded on economics which few of them understood. The colonies had been left to their own devices too long to allow Parliament to interfere, however minutely. This was the opinion of the wealthy, influential men who first conceived the notion of independence from Britain and who then incited the people to war. But it would be common men and women with idealistic principles who would fight for and achieve the creation of a nation.

2 THE CALL TO ARMS

Although an armed confrontation between colonists and British troops had occurred there were few outside Massachusetts who understood precisely what was transpiring or why. The New England colonies obviously believed that an impasse had been reached but the situation was not yet one of revolution nor even war. The colonists still considered themselves Englishmen who were merely defending their rights as such. It might almost be said that the situation around Boston was more along the lines of civil disorder, or perhaps a minor civil war.

As colonists from Vermont, New Hampshire, Rhode Island and New York made their way toward Boston the Second Continental Congress convened in Philadelphia, Pennsylvania, in May 1775. The primary issue lay in what action should next be taken. Northern delegates such as Samuel Adams and Patrick Henry called upon the membership to declare their independence from the Crown. They encouraged the Congress to approach France and Spain for assistance, particularly military goods which were in short supply. However, most of the delegates were more conservative and reluctant to break from England. John Dickinson, a Pennsylvanian who led the conservative faction, convinced the Congress to send assurances to King George III that there were no ambitious designs in the colonies for separation from England and to seek a reconciliation with Parliament. To appease the more radical element the conservatives added that, although they believed a solution could be found, they would not permit the previous conditions to persist nor would they hesitate to resist tyranny with force if necessary. To illustrate their determination George Washington was appointed as Commander in Chief of the Continental Army. In a sense this appointment placed Washington in command of something which did not truly exist, as the only 'army' the colonies possessed was the militia. The Congress hoped their action would convince King George of their sincerity.

Political maneuvers were not the only ones being made. In Massachusetts General Ward was placed in command of the forces surrounding Boston. As leaders in Massachusetts rallied support from other colonies they created an unprecedented situation by commissioning Captain Benedict Arnold of the Connecticut militia as a colonel of Massachusetts. The purpose of this commission was to raise a force of 400 men from various colonies to attack and capture the British Fort Ticonderoga on Lake Champlain in New York. This first combined colonial militia gave credence to the claims that the individual colonies were now becoming part of a unified whole. Although the union was for the moment loose and unofficial the implication was clear. Arnold organized his force and set out for Ticonderoga. En route he was joined by a militia unit from Vermont known as the Green Mountain Boys under the command of Ethan Allen.

As the Continental Congress was meeting Arnold and Allen attacked Fort Ticonderoga. Their surprise assault caught the British garrison completely off guard and the fort was taken almost without a shot being fired. The capture was a great prize, not only because of the strategic location of the fort but for the military supplies which were captured, which included 80 artillery pieces. These guns would be the basis on which the colonists would build their artillery force. The majority of the powder and shot captured was sent immediately to Boston to be followed by the slower moving artillery.

Before these stores could reach Boston General Gage decided to take action against the Colonial forces. On 15 June the Provisional Committee for the Safety of the Massachusetts Colony had ordered General Ward to occupy the strategic heights around the city and its bay. The Committee had specifically directed Ward and his militia to move to the hills at Dorchester south of the city at the entrance of Boston Harbor and to Bunker Hill which lay on the Charlestown peninsula north of the city across the harbor. From these points the colonists believed they could make the British position in Boston intolerable, forcing them to withdraw to their ships and return to Halifax. Although the colonists had no cannon larger than six pounders, they had a commanding position from which to bombard Boston if they so desired. Both the colonial and British commands realized the importance of the positions.

On the afternoon of 16 June 1775 militia general Israel Putnam issued orders for a colonial force of approximately 1000 men to march to and secure the heights. The British had been considering a similar

Above: Ethan Allen demands the surrender of Fort Ticonderoga from the British commander, Captain de la Place.
Right: Israel Putnam, one of the leading colonial commanders in the battles around Boston.
Below: The powder captured at Fort Ticonderoga is transported to Boston for use at Bunker Hill.

maneuver but on that night General Clinton, who had been conducting reconnaissance in the area north of Charlestown, reported to Gage that the colonists had already moved to the heights. He suggested that they should reconsider their own strategy. However, Gage did not agree with Clinton's plan to land troops behind Bunker Hill. Instead he decided that the best course of action would be a direct approach, moving his forces directly across the bay to land at Morton's Point. From there they would assault the hills. Gage was confident that he could succeed as he had several important points in his favor. By landing farther along the Charlestown Peninsula rather than at Charlestown itself he could use the high ground at Morton's Hill for his artillery thus compensating for the colonists' position. By shifting his forces to the center and right he could also employ Admiral Graves' naval guns and the British artillery on Copp's Hill, Boston, for support. Finally, in spite of the wariness felt for the colonial riflemen after the Concord incident, Gage was confident that an assault by formed British regulars would be far more than the colonists could withstand. Casualties might be heavy but the battle would last only as long as it took the regulars to take the hills and

rout the colonists.

The colonists' plan was simply to defend. After taking Bunker Hill Putnam and Colonel Prescott decided to move their main force to Breed's Hill which afforded a greater field of vision and range of fire over the plains between the heights and Charlestown. Breed's Hill was lower and perhaps would be more easily assaulted, but they considered its advantages would outweigh this fact.

On the morning of 17 June the British naval guns and the Copp's Hill batteries began a barrage of Breed's Hill. In an amazingly short time the colonists had constructed fortifications atop Breed's Hill and Gage decided that he must attack quickly. From those early shots until 1200 hours British troops assembled on the Boston Commons to cross the bay. Putnam and Prescott used the time well, improving their defenses. The British cannon fire had for the most part fallen short of the colonists defenses as the naval vessels could not get adequate elevation to strike accurately. Still the cannonade had begun to unnerve the weary colonists. Putnam realized that their resolve had begun to waver and he and Prescott urged the men on. Their efforts to maintain discipline were almost destroyed when Prescott's men were thrown into shocked confusion as a round from the British guns ricocheted along the top of the hill decapitating one of the young colonists. The men panicked, unaccustomed to such battlefield horror. Prescott screamed orders, realizing that his command was in danger of collapse but the body held the attention of the men and as some stood immobilized others threw down their tools and ran toward Bunker Hill away from the front. Finally Prescott leaped to the top of the wood and earth defense works exposing himself to the artillery fire to show his men that there was really nothing to fear. Other officers joined him at points along the defense. The men finally began to work once more but the air of near mutiny was apparent. Prescott continued to drive them, walking all along the fortifications.

British troops had begun to arrive and were forming some 800 yards below Prescott's position. He realized that if the position was to be held, reinforcements would have to be brought forward. Unknown to

Left: George Washington takes command of the Continental Army outside Boston. Washington was chosen partly for his experience as a militia commander in the French and Indian War and partly for political reasons.
Below: A contemporary print shows the Battle of Bunker Hill and the burning of Charlestown.

Prescott, Putnam had left the hills for that purpose. Putnam went to General Ward with his request for reinforcements but Ward was unwilling to respond. He feared that the British would make their way up the river to Cambridge where the colonial command and the main supply depot were situated. Finally, convinced that the British were making their move against the peninsula hills, he released 1200 men of the two New Hampshire regiments to take a position along a wood and stone wall on Prescott's left. Later he would add more militia and artillery to bolster the position.

At 1500 hours the initial British force under General Howe and a reserve he had requested were landed and prepared to attack. The force consisted of 13 companies of grenadiers, 13 companies of light infantry, six battalions of regular line infantry and detachments of Royal Artillery. The assault began when Howe sent his light infantry on an abrupt flanking maneuver against the colonists holding the left wall. John Stark commanded the colonial forces there. Before the attack he had sent several men 40 yards ahead of his position to pound reference stakes into the ground. Stark knew that he had 200 of the finest frontiersmen from New Hampshire in his ranks who at 40 yards would have such deadly accuracy that no British soldier could possibly advance

CHARLES TOWN

BOSTON

further. He deployed his men in three lines ready to fire volleys. The British advance reached the markers and the first colonial volley dropped the leading infantry line almost to a man. Successive rounds annhilated the light infantry. The bodies were so numerous that the red coats of the infantry hid the ground. Their advance was broken. Behind the light infantry Howe sent his main attack in two massive lines, three ranks deep. British artillery at Morton's Hill were to support this awesome advance. However, when the reserve ammunition boxes were opened it was discovered that 12-pound shot instead of the necessary 6-pound shot had been mistakenly supplied. Howe was furious but he ordered the guns brought forward so that they could use grapeshot.

As the British troops climbed Breed's Hill the colonists waited. Putnam rode along his lines steadying the men and ordering them to hold their fire until they could 'see the whites of their eyes'. When the grenadiers were within 30 yards of the colonial defenses the order to fire was given. One thousand colonial muskets fired, quickly followed by a second devastating volley. The grenadiers broke, falling back to the bottom of the hill. The colonists had easily won the first round. Howe considered this only a momentary setback and ordered his men to form for another assault. Several of his officers argued against this as losses had already been enormous. Nevertheless Howe had been ordered to secure the hills and he intended to do so.

However, Putnam's forces were facing a major dilemma. Most of the colonists had arrived for the battle with fewer than 13 rounds of ammunition each and although they scavenged among their own dead and wounded Putnam realized that they had only enough powder and shot for two or three more volleys.

As the British units formed for a second assault their losses became even more apparent. Companies called to form ranks discovered that they had only a handful of men remaining. The losses were most apparent in the grenadier units. The situation was indeed critical. Howe recognized despair on the faces of his grenadiers and as a military man he realized that his army had reached the fine line which divides discipline from chaos. This made it even more important for his forces to renew their assault and accomplish their objective no matter how great the cost. With the addition of his reserves Howe launched his final attack against Prescott's position at 1730 hours. The colonial commanders realized that this assault would probably overwhelm them but with a little luck they might break the British morale with the volleys they could fire. Prescott moved along the line ordering his men to hold their fire. The 30-yard stakes were soon tramped under by the advancing line. At 20 yards the order to fire was given. The results were as devastating as they had been in the initial attack but the British officers drove their forces forward. Prescott knew that his position was lost.

The British 47th Regiment and two companies of marines were the first to reach the fortification. The melee was brief and bloody as the colonists had no response to the British bayonets. Although many of the colonists attempted to stand and fight they were no match for British regulars at close quarters and Prescott ordered a retreat. Although a few of his force were left as a rear guard, Prescott's retreat had a note of panic as the men feared that the British might push forward and massacre them. However, the British had reached their limit. Their honor was intact and they no longer wished to pursue the fight. Older, experienced officers claimed that the effort to take Breed's Hill involved fighting worse than any they had seen, even on the battlefields in Europe.

Elsewhere the British line advanced, capturing the wall on the colonists' left flank and continuing on toward Bunker Hill. Although Putnam organized a final defense at Bunker Hill the situation was hopeless and he ordered his force to withdraw. Of the 1800 colonists who saw action 145 were killed and 304 wounded, most of the casualties occurring during the final melee. The British casualty list was far longer. Of the 2600 men sent against the colonial positions, 1100 became casualties with 250 killed. Eighty-nine officers were killed or wounded. The battle was over but the two forces continued to face one another. The colonists had the British blocked into the peninsula and considered their defense at Breed's Hill a victory. They had inflicted a great deal of damage on Howe's force and had not actually been driven from the hills but had merely run short of ammunition.

On 2 July General George Washington assumed command of militia operations in the Boston region. He continued to tighten the encirclement around the British and spent the remaining months of 1775 training the colonial forces. Recruitment and discipline were primary concerns if the militia was to fulfill its role as the first Continental Army. Early in 1776 Washington surprised the British command by moving his forces into the heights at Dorchester, which had for some reason been overlooked by the British. Although when he took the heights Washington had little influence over the city or channel, by early March he had moved artillery into a position from which he could command those areas. The guns supplied were those from Ticonderoga which Colonel Henry Knox had moved on sleds through the winter snow to Boston. With cannon overlooking the mouth of the bay and the city Howe, who had replaced Gage as commander of British forces in Boston, decided it was useless to attempt to hold on and risk a military disaster. The entire British garrison and 1000 Loyalists, or Tories as the colonists described them, were evacuated from Boston. The colonists had won their first notable victory.

3 WASHINGTON TURNS THE TIDE

Above: Benedict Arnold (1741–1801) served with distinction in the advance into Canada but later joined the British.

Although Boston had been the center of attention it was not the only area where the colonists and British had come into conflict. On 6 June 1775 a separate colonial 'army' was formed with responsibility for securing the frontier between the colonies and Canada. Although there were those who feared that the Canadians might assist the British there were many leaders who thought that since much of Canada had only recently been conquered by Britain the French people there might join in the colonial movement against the Crown. Before the Canadians could be convinced to aid the colonies a victory in the area would have to be attained to prove that the colonists could indeed defeat the British army.

Several officers were commissioned by the Con-

tinental Congress, not by their individual colonies, to accomplish this goal. On 30 August 1775 a force under Brigadier General Richard Montgomery and General Philip Schuyler advanced toward Montreal from Ticonderoga along the traditional northern route past Lake George and Lake Champlain. This force, of which General Schuyler was primary commander, consisted of 1800 men. At the same time Washington, acting independent of the Continental Congress, decided to send a force under General Benedict Arnold by sea to the Kennebec River. From there it was to make its way to Quebec. Washington believed that this two pronged attack against Canada would put an added strain on Sir Guy Carleton, military governor of the region. Carleton would be forced to decide which city he would defend. If Washington's plan functioned properly Carleton would find himself caught between the two forces and unable adequately to defend either city. Arnold set out with more than 1000 volunteers from the forces gathered around Boston.

On 6 September Schuyler laid siege to St Johns, just outside Montreal, but a nagging illness later forced him to relinquish command. This was fortunate as Montgomery was actually the more able officer. The garrison of St Johns capitulated on 2 November but Carleton escaped with part of his force to retreat toward Quebec. On 13 November Montreal was occupied by the colonial forces. During that time Arnold was being harassed not only by the British but by intolerable weather and terrain which nearly destroyed his small army. On 9 November he reached the outskirts of Quebec with only little more than 600 men, most of whom were exhausted after their difficult trek. Montgomery, with a force of only 300 men, was not able to join Arnold at Quebec until 31 December. As their force lacked sufficient numbers to attack the Quebec garrison openly, Arnold and Montgomery decided to assault the walled city during a snow storm. The assault achieved initial success but collapsed when Montgomery was killed and Arnold seriously wounded. In spite of the failure Arnold refused to relinquish his goal. He combined the remnants of the two forces and laid siege to Quebec calling on the Continental Congress for reinforcements. His siege, though heroic was somewhat

foolhardy. The men suffered throughout the long winter while inside the city Carleton had only to wait for spring. Hunger and exposure were Arnold's principal enemies. To make matters worse smallpox broke out in the camp. Although Washington and the Congress planned to send reinforcements to Arnold in the spring of 1776 those plans were thwarted when the British sent 10,000 troops under the command of General Burgoyne up the St Lawrence to break the siege.

During that winter the rebellion had also extended to the southern colonies. On 20 January General Clinton sailed from New England with a force of approximately 1500 men to rendezvous with another force under the command of General Lord Charles Cornwallis off Cape Fear, North Carolina. Cornwallis had come from Ireland with a fleet commanded by Admiral Parker. Originally their combined force was bound for Charleston, South Carolina, to put down the growing unrest in that area. On the request of Governor Josiah Martin of North Carolina Corn-wallis' course was altered and he joined with Clinton at Cape Fear. Martin had convinced the British that several Loyalist Tory regiments could be raised in North Carolina which would then join with the British in quelling the rebellions being staged in South Carolina and Georgia. Martin had in fact begun to raise an army from the Piedmont area of North Carolina and by 14 February assembled a force of 700 Scots Highlanders and 800 other Loyalists under the command of Donald McDonald, a capable old soldier in his eighties. No sooner had this force been raised than other colonists, now calling themselves Patriots, raised a regiment of more than 1000 volunteers with which to meet the British along the coast.

On 27 February at Moore's Creek Bridge McDonald's Tories clashed with Patriots for the first battle in the southern colonies. To the sound of pipes and drums the Tories attacked the Patriots, screaming 'King George and Broadswords.' The battle ended almost as quickly as it was begun as the Tory troops met the withering fire of the frontier riflemen. Their retreat soon turned to rout as the Patriots counter-attacked. Over the following 48 hours more than 800 Tory troops were captured, preventing any possibility of a rendezvous with the British force. It was a moral victory for the Patriot's cause which dampened open support for the Loyalist movement.

On 12 April the North Carolina Assembly instructed its delegates to the Second Continental Congress to rescind its former decision to remain a colony of the Crown, joining those who advocated independence. It was the first colony to take an official stance on the issue. When news of this reached the British forces in North Carolina the command immediately returned the troops to their vessels and set sail for their original destination, Charleston.

Clinton rejected the suggestion that he return to New York City, where Howe had moved his army. Instead he went south with Cornwallis. Clinton intended to return north once Charleston was secured. With Clinton to aid him Cornwallis was certain that he could achieve a swift, decisive victory in South Carolina. However, the Patriots in that area had not been idly waiting for the British to arrive. The entrance to Charleston harbor was protected by fortifications on two small islands; Fort Johnson on James Island and Fort Sullivan, later to be known as Fort Moultrie, on Sullivan Island. Fort Sullivan, which was only partially completed and virtually open in the rear was indefensible by all standards yet Colonel Moultrie with fewer than 400 men withstood the bombardment of more than 100 British naval guns. Three warships had closed upon the island and Moultrie's men succeeded in damaging all three and causing more than 200 British casualties. Clinton then attempted a naval assault, landing most of his force on the nearby Long Island, or Isle of Palms. The islands were separated by a narrow channel which Clinton had been led to believe would be easily forded. As his troops attempted to cross the channel it was quickly discovered that the information given had been false. The water was more than seven feet deep, not 18 inches

as was believed. Clinton's attack was broken. By
nightfall the battle itself was over. The Patriots had
lost only 40 men, killed or wounded. Clinton, his
casualty rate high as a result of the assault attempt,
embarked his troops the following morning and sailed
for New York to join Howe. These two engagements
and the colonial victories they produced would keep
the southern colonies free of British control for the
next three years.

The winter and early spring of 1776 had been an
eventful period. In the spring the Continental
Congress met to debate the question of independence
and George Washington moved his army to New
York. He believed that if the British were able to hold
that city they could use it as a base for land and naval
operations, seriously endangering the colonial position in New England. By July Washington had more
than 20,000 men in the city and surrounding countryside. On 2 July the Continental Congress voted to
declare the colonies independent of England, no
longer referring to themselves as colonial Englishmen
but as Americans. On the same day General Lord
William Howe sailed into New York harbor and
landed troops on Staten Island. Howe's army consisted of more than 30,000 British regulars and a
large proportion of Hessian troops who were now
fighting as mercenaries for the British. Several days
later his brother, Admiral Lord Howe, moved his
powerful fleet into the harbor to reinforce the troop
maneuvers. By August they were prepared to begin
their campaign against George Washington and New
York.

In mid August General Howe took approximately
20,000 men and attacked Brooklyn Heights on Long
Island. The heights were defended by General
Putnam, who like so many others had left Boston to
protect New York. Putnam shared his command with
General John Sullivan, who was in immediate
command on the day the British chose to attack. As
Howe maneuvered troops against the heights he also
began a maneuver against the Americans' left flank
while Admiral Howe sailed his warships to a point
from which to bombard the Brooklyn fortification
and block any avenue of retreat for the American
forces. General Howe's maneuver was brilliantly
executed, catching the Americans completely by
surprise. In the first day he not only cleared the ridge
of defenders but inflicted more than 1500 casualties
while suffering fewer than 400 himself. The only thing
that saved the American troops from complete
destruction was a change in the weather. Swift tides
caught Admiral Howe's fleet, forcing it to move away
from its supporting position.

By late afternoon on 27 August the American troops
who escaped the earlier destruction had moved to the
safety of the Brooklyn fortification but it took the
appearance of George Washington on the scene with
reinforcements from New York to stabilize the
situation. Washington prepared plans for a counterattack but realized that his troops would be unable to
see it through and concentrated instead on a defensive
posture. Without the support of the warships General
Howe took a more conservative stance, preparing to
lay an active siege. The memory of the devastating
firepower brought against British troops at Breed's
and Bunker Hills was still clear and the men were not
anxious to assault colonial fortifications again. Washington realized that his position was untenable,

knowing that only the storms had kept the British from advancing, and ordered a retreat across the East River. Under cover of fog and darkness the American troops were able to reach Manhattan Island. If Howe had been able to trap and destroy Washington's forces at Staten Island the American Revolution might well have ended at that point.

Howe then lost two weeks in fruitless talks with the Continental Congress, which had sent a committee to discuss the possibility of peace negotiations. When he finally admitted that the talks were futile Howe renewed his attack by landing troops on Manhattan Island at Kip's Bay. He hoped the landing there would enable him to isolate Washington from the troops he had left in the city and force him to abandon New York. The American force fled along the western edge of the island, halting only when they had reached Harlem Heights. There they stood to defend. Howe executed another flanking maneuver, on this occasion landing troops at Throg's Neck, but this failed as the American troops had destroyed an essential bridge. Howe attempted another landing at Pell's Point but Washington countered this effort by retreating to White Plains. He left a force of approximately 5000 men behind under the command of General Nathaniel Greene at Fort Washington at the northern tip of Manhattan Island and Fort Lee, across the Hudson River on the Palisades in New Jersey.

In response to Washington's action Howe maneuvered again and attacked Washington on 28 October, successfully capturing the hills around White Plains. The loss of these strategic hills forced Washington to withdraw to a new position five miles to the north at North Castle. Washington was attempting to draw Howe away from the city, but the British general was not so easily led. Howe had forced Washington to separate his forces from those left behind at the forts. Turning away from Washington Howe moved south, attacking Fort Washington and isolating it from the other American forces. General Washington had waited too long to order the evacuation of the forts. In an overwhelming assault Howe's troops captured Fort Washington and its 3000-man garrison. Two days later Howe sent another command of 5000 men under General Cornwallis across the river for a surprise attack on Fort Lee. The attack came so quickly that Greene and his garrison barely escaped.

With the forts lost and his army out of position Washington was forced to retreat to New Jersey. He moved south to the Delaware River to establish a defensive position which would offer protection against an advance on the American capital of Philadelphia. By the time Washington and his army crossed the Delaware, Howe had suspended operations to prepare winter quarters in New York. As well as the troubles in the New York area the Americans

were suffering harsh reverses elsewhere. After Arnold's initial failure at Quebec the Americans put together a 15-ship flotilla on Lake Champlain to await the British counterattack from Canada. On 11 October 1776 25 British vessels engaged the American flotilla in a five-hour battle, during which the Americans lost two vessels. The British fleet then anchored across the channel in the belief that they had trapped the Americans. In a daring night maneuver the American vessels escaped to a position 10 miles away before the British were aware of the move. Sir Guy Carleton, commander of the fleet forces, chased Arnold and his flotilla.

When they met again two more American vessels

Below: The Battle of Valcour Island, 11 October 1776. The British ships (from left) *Maria*, *Carleton* and *Inflexible*.

Above: Marines from Arnold's ships wade ashore after they have been beached following the defeat at Valcour Island and the subsequent British pursuit.

were destroyed in combat and two others beached and burned. Arnold landed his army and set out overland toward Crown Point. Although the American force had suffered during this engagement they had delayed Carleton long enough to force him to call a halt to his campaign. Rather than pursue Arnold, Carleton laid siege to Fort Ticonderoga where he expected to meet Howe's forces advancing from New York. However, Howe had concentrated his full efforts against Washington and when Carleton discovered that Howe was not coming to his aid he broke off his siege and returned to Canada for the winter.

By the time he had crossed the Delaware for the winter of 1776–77 Washington found his command had been reduced to 3000 men. Morale was extremely low and he realized that he must make an effort to not only boost morale but to gain supplies for his army. The Continental Congress seemed unwilling or unable to respond to his requests for provisions and materiel. Washington decided that the best source of those items would be the British army. It was already a harsh winter, about which Thomas Paine would write, 'This was the time that would try men's souls. The summer soldier and sunshine patriot will, in this crisis, shrink from the service of their country; but he that stands it now deserves the love and thanks of all men and women.' Paine's words, though inspiring, were a severe rebuke to those who had deserted the ranks to return home when the balance weighed heavily in Britain's favor. Desertion was perhaps Washington's worst enemy but he refused to allow himself to become pessimistic. He devised a strategy which with the reinforcements gained by the addition of General John Cadwalader's and General Ewing's forces would enable him to strike back at the British and offset the effects of the New York campaign.

On 23 December Washington made plans to attack the Hessian garrison at Trenton, New Jersey, just across the Delaware River. On Christmas Eve he met with his officers at General Greene's headquarters to outline their assault. General Hitchock's Rhode Islanders and 2000 Pennsylvania militia under General Cadwalader were to cross the river at Bristol to convince Colonel von Donop's Hessian brigade that the Americans intended to attack their position at Burlington. The second phase of Washington's three-pronged offensive was the movement of General Ewing's 1000-man brigade across the river at Trenton Ferry. There Ewing would block the avenue of retreat for the Hessian garrison at Trenton and also act as a guard to prevent von Donop from escaping Cadwalader's ploy and reinforcing Trenton. The third phase of the operation would be commanded by Washington himself. With approximately 2500 men and 18 cannon he intended to cross the Delaware seven or eight miles north of Trenton at a point known as McKonkey's Ferry. He would then swing toward Trenton from the north in two columns, enveloping

the town. This was all to occur on Christmas Day.

On 25 December Washington moved his troops to the ferry points and waited for darkness to avoid detection by Hessian scouts who might be patrolling the area. The Hessian commander at Trenton, Colonel Johan Rall, was known not only as an above average commander but as a man prone to excesses and frivolity. Washington was assuming that the Hessian garrison would be celebrating that evening and that their pickets and patrols would be somewhat lax. His assumption was correct. Rall had placed his grenadier company on guard that evening but it was a token gesture as he and his officers were all attending a party given by one of Trenton's Loyalist citizens. He did not even consider the possibility of an attack from Washington's forces as it was assumed that the Americans would wait until spring before attempting further operations.

At 2300 hours on 25 December Washington's troops began crossing the Delaware but a storm interrupted the maneuver and the last of his forces were not able to cross until 0300 hours on the 26th. Knox's artillery followed one hour later. Although Washington took every precaution to keep the crossing secret a Loyalist farmer on the Trenton side of the Delaware noticed the congregation of soldiers and rushed to Trenton to warn Rall of an impending attack. Fortunately for the American troops when the farmer arrived in Trenton he was denied permission to see Rall, sent away with the rebuke that the colonel was enjoying himself too much to be concerned with idle rumors. By 0400 hours Washington had formed his army three and one-half miles north of Trenton and was prepared to advance. At 0730 Greene's column encountered Hessian pickets on the Pennington Road. The pickets, who numbered less than 17, formed ranks to repel what they believed was nothing more than a small band of Patriots sent to harass them. As volleys were exchanged it became evident to the picket commander that a major force confronted him. His troops broke and raced to Trenton to sound the alarm.

It was, however, too late. The Americans had moved round the town and the bulk of Washington's force was moving against the disorganized Hessian garrison. Although 400 Hessians crossed the Asunpink Bridge before Washington could seal off that escape route, Ewing's militia blocked their path. The Hessians made a desperate attempt to hold the town but the element of surprise had irreversibly swung the balance in Washington's favor. Within an hour 1000 Hessian troops were captured. Rall was mortally wounded. He lived only long enough to surrender his sword to General Washington. The victory at Trenton was overwhelming, with only five American casualties, and the morale of the army soared.

Nonetheless Washington could not afford to pause. His small army was vulnerable to attack from Princeton or Bordentown. The British had reinforced

Above: Washington Crossing the Delaware, after the painting by Emanuel Leutze. Although obviously not an accurate representation of the incident it gives a vivid impression of the wintry conditions prevailing.
Right: The mortally wounded Colonel Rall surrenders his sword to Washington.

that area and by 2 January 1777 Cornwallis was en route to Trenton. That night he halted outside the city and seeing the campfires burning remarked that he 'had the fox in the trap.' Considering the colonial commanders to be less qualified than himself, Cornwallis was confident that he could crush Washington's force in the morning and ordered his own troops to bivouac. Several of his officers disagreed, urging the general to push on and attack while he had the colonists in an exposed position, but Cornwallis rejected their proposals. In fact Washington had taken

few chances and his pickets noted the arrival of the British army and its bivouac preparations. Washington realized that he was outnumbered and facing some of the best British troops. He embarked on a bold strategy, ordering his officers to go among the men directing them to make their fires as large as possible and for the men on the outer perimeter to make as much noise as possible without being foolishly obvious. Washington planned to put Cornwallis at ease and while maintaining the charade move his army around the British flank. By dawn he hoped to be

Above: The death of Mercer at the Battle of Princeton, 3 January 1777. The British 17th Regiment only saved themselves from annihilation by a vigorous bayonet charge.

well north of Cornwallis at Princeton, thus escaping the trap and severing the British lines of supply and communication at the same time.

The plan worked well until Washington's forces were almost within reach of Princeton. There a British force led by Lieutenant Colonel Charles Mawhood intercepted the American advance. Mawhood's 17th and 55th Regiments were marching to join Cornwallis while his 40th Regiment remained behind in Princeton to guard the stores there. At 0800 hours the 17th Regiment had just crossed Stoney Brook at Worth's Mill when they became aware that Washington was maneuvering around their left flank. The 17th Regiment raced back toward a hilltop between Stoney Brook and Princeton to block Washington's unsuspecting forces. In the running battle with the 17th Regiment that ensued Brigadier General Hugh Mercer's and Cadwalader's brigades were almost broken when panic started in Cadwalader's force began to spread to Mercer's men. Washington realized that if the panic spread the battle would be lost and embarked on a course which would earn him the status of both hero and glorious leader. He rode recklessly between the British and American lines to rally his men. As he rode volleys were fired by both the lines. Washington's aide, Colonel Fitzgerald, was certain that his commander had been killed. Before the smoke from the first volley cleared the 17th fired again. Suddenly Washington appeared, riding out of the smoke, urging his troops to stand fast and return the fire. The army took heart as other officers rode forward following Washington's example. Mawhood realized that if he did not attempt to counterattack the 17th Regiment would be lost. He ordered a

charge and as the 17th rushed forward they were overwhelmed by the volleys brought to bear against them. Mawhood's men panicked and routed.

Washington himself led the pursuit. At Princeton Mawhood discovered that his forces there had made a brief stand but were falling back rapidly under fire from the American artillery. The battle for Princeton was virtually over. As the Americans continued to advance the British brigade fled the city. British losses were heavy but Washington had only six officers and 30 men killed. The number wounded was never accurately recorded, primarily to make the victory with so few deaths seem more decisive. Mawhood would later report that his casualties were approximately 18 killed, 100 wounded and 200 captured. Although those were the official figures they were probably an extreme understatement as American reports later indicated that on 4 January Washington's men buried the British dead in 18 common graves with as many as 21 British soldiers in each.

When Cornwallis heard the battle to his rear and his advance guard informed him that Washington had escaped, he withdrew to Brunswick to protect his supply base, thus forcing the British lines on the whole back to New York. Howe was forced to react accordingly by withdrawing from New Jersey.

From Princeton Washington moved north to establish winter quarters in the hills around Morristown. Such victories were crucial at a time when the British thought the colonists were on the verge of collapse. Washington had secured all but the northeastern section of the colonies and many of those who thought the army lost came back into the ranks. Morale and enlistment rates were the highest they had ever been. Washington could train his growing army during the winter, viewing the new year with optimism. His gamble in New Jersey had kept the Revolution alive.

4 INDEPENDENCE DECLARED

have been served nor a better form of life achieved.

It also became apparent to the rebellious leaders that although many colonists were unhappy with the recent course of events, support for the movement against the Crown was far from overwhelming. Perhaps one-third of the colonists supported the

Left: A statue of George III is pulled down by a group of colonists. It was later melted down to make bullets.
Below: The colonial leader Patrick Henry addresses a meeting.

The year 1776 was important on the battlefield but the political maneuvers made were monumental. In the spring the colonists were still refusing to admit that they were fighting a war with Britain, insisting that it was merely an effort to preserve their rights which forced them to take up arms. Many claimed that the independence of the colonies had been declared when the first shots were fired at Lexington but the majority were reluctant to sever the bonds which held them to Britain. The most convincing argument in favor of reconcilation was that it had been the Crown and the British Army which had kept law and order and maintained stability in the colonies, which in turn resulted in the prosperity that was enjoyed. Without Britain's ruling hand to bind them, many believed that the colonies would revert to mob rule and anarchy, breaking into 13 individual nations. There were those who argued that if the colonies broke from Britain the groundwork would be laid for individual states and principalities to form as had been the case in Europe. Eventually such a situation would lead to conflict between those states and no purpose would

radical position taken by men like Adams, Henry and Hancock. Another third supported a Loyalist position and many of them rallied to support the British forces. The remaining one-third of the population viewed both the radicals and the conservatives with equal disdain, wanting no part in the conflict. They saw no benefit in advocating either stance and wanted most to return to the days prior to the 'Stamp Act.'

Perhaps the most personal reason for the unwillingness of the colonial legislators to declare independence was their lack of confidence in the ability of the colonies to achieve that independence. If the rebellion failed they would be executed for treason. They had powerful support in Parliament in such men as Isaac Barre, Edmund Burke, William Pitt and John Wilkes who saw the colonies as more than a market place or dumping ground for undesirables. British merchants had added their support, appealing to Parliament to solve the problems which were having a serious effect on their profits in the Americas. However, two bitter facts continued to surface. Regardless of arguments brought forward by conservatives or the love loyal colonists might feel for Britain, no one could deny that Parliament had acted in a manner which disregarded the colonists' rights. The fact that they were not granted the same privileges as British citizens resident in Britain had been implanted in the minds of the colonists as an intolerable circumstance. The second fact which could not be ignored, and which was repeatedly brought forward by the radicals, was that colonial blood had been spilled after the British made the first aggressive gesture by marching on Lexington and Concord. Adams maintained that the British had fired first, and thus that the Crown had begun the conflict.

As the debate on the issues of independence continued colonists took opposing stands with deep and equal conviction. Thomas Paine gave the most logical, and convincing argument for a declaration of independence. He pointed out that once the colonies declared their independence citizens who joined the armies against the Crown would be treated as prisoners of war and not as traitors who could be shot or hanged immediately. The government of the independent colonies could by rights seize the property of Loyalist activists, thereby providing revenue for the government and the revolution. As an independent government, not just colonies in revolt, the Congress could approach foreign governments for aid and support. Representatives had already traveled to the courts of France and Spain and were encouraged by the signs of favor they received.

In the aftermath of Paine's remarks on 7 June 1776 Richard Henry Lee, a Congressional representative from Virginia, introduced a resolution stating that the colonies were united and had the right to be declared free and independent states. Four days later that resolution was brought to a vote at the Second Continental Congress and adopted. The Congress appointed a five member committee to draft a formal declaration of independence. Of the five Thomas Jefferson was considered the most capable and became the chief architect of the document. The other four members were Benjamin Franklin, John Adams, the less radical of the Adams brothers, Robert Livingston and Roger Sherman.

On 28 June the committee returned to the Continental Congress with the draft of the document. As presented the delegates could not accept the document and a debate of its contents ensued, allegedly on the grounds of debating Lee's initial resolution to declare independence. The Congress reviewed the document paragraph by paragraph, adding and deleting words and phrases but essentially the document was not changed. Jefferson's vehement condemnation of King George III was removed, as was his reference to the illegality of the slave trade. That latter point was a source of heated debate. Jefferson saw it as an integral part of the concept of freedom, in spite of the fact that he was himself a slave owner, but the delegates

Above: A copy of the Declaration of Independence.
Above left: The flag of the newly created United States is saluted at the signing of the Declaration.
Below left: The Declaration is read to Washington's army.

and merchants from the northern colonies had financial ties with the slave trade and the southern delegates and plantation owners depended on slavery for their continued prosperity. Half way through the debate Franklin had to pacify and console Jefferson who claimed that the delegates were destroying his efforts. Finally on 4 July 1776 the Congress officially adopted the final draft of the Declaration of Independence. Led by John Hancock, president of the Congress, the document was signed. One copy each was sent to King George and Parliament then other copies were dispatched to the different legislative bodies throughout the colonies, which had suddenly become States of the Union.

Four days later the document was read in a proclamation in Philadelphia, the new nation's capital. Reactions were mixed. The Patriots, who had referred to themselves by that name, or as Whigs, and now as Americans, viewed the document as an assurance of America's future freedom. Those who had not previously aligned themselves to any faction reacted to the document with indifference as the ravings of radicals. The Loyalist Tory element was put in a dangerously precarious position. The Declaration described their loyalty to Britain as traitorous to the land they now claimed as their home. Many feared

for their lives and property. The declaration was not one of freedom for this sector of the population but was a decree which would pit neighbor against neighbor and family members against one another.

The Declaration of Independence itself incorporated all the points which had been made during the past several years. The Preamble gave the reasons, 27 in all, for the separation which was being made. It also depicted King George as a tyrant and the people of the colonies as sufferers under his rule. It laid out the basic theories for the establishment of a new government given the consideration that 'all men are created equal' with the 'inalienable rights' of 'Life, Liberty, and the Pursuit of Happiness.' Jefferson laid out the responsibility of the new government to protect and uphold those rights, governing only with the consent of the people. It called upon all men of all times to rid themselves of tyrants, and finally it was a formal declaration of war between the United States of America and Britain.

It is important to discuss for whom this document was written. As it appeared it declared itself as a revolutionary doctrine for all people. With the acknowledgement of the principles set forth the radical rebellion of a few blossomed into a movement of the common citizens. The revolution was no longer confined to the merchant or upper class to whom the economic issues were of primary importance, nor the radical politicians who saw the license they had been granted suddenly being curtailed. The revolution was suddenly an ideal which promised something greater than had ever been. No aspect of society would be excluded from the movement which the Declaration set in motion. All would play a role in fighting for the cause. Colonists of every ethnic background rallied in support of the revolution, not because they despised the King or Britain, but because it represented that which they had come to the colonies to find – freedom. No one religious group acknowledged or denied the movement as Catholics, Protestants and even Quakers rallied in support. This point was extremely important as wars in Europe had so often been fought on boundaries set by religious convictions. The Quakers, who were forbidden by their belief to bear arms, contributed to the revolution with financial aid, supplies and in non-combat roles.

Perhaps most importantly the spirit of freedom and independence brought a response which was not confined to white, Christian males. In 1778 George Washington was empowered to raise a force of more than 400 Indians to serve as scouts for the Continental Army. There have been disparaging allegations that the support given to the Revolution by American Indians was done for the reward or payment they received. This narrow theory is dispelled by the evidence that American Indians remained with the Continental Army at Valley Forge, freezing to death alongside the colonists rather than abandon the

SEE BLACKS IN B.G

concept of freedom which they so clearly understood. Of the 2000 Jews in the colonies almost all supported the revolution, the most noted being Haym Salomon who helped the new nation find the finances to carry on the war and later helped the Congress find funds with which to back the first government.

Blacks also played an important role, whether they were freemen or slaves, as they fought alongside white troops in the early militia units. Crispus Attucks one of the first to die in the 'Boston Massacre' presented an example which many would follow. Peter Salem a black militia soldier at Bunker Hill was credited with killing Major Pitcairn at the battle. Although the Continental Congress later barred blacks from enlisting in the Continental Army, due to pressures brought by southern delegates, Washington rescinded that order, accepting any black who wanted to fight. Eventually he forced the Congress to revoke its prohibition on black enlistments. This is not to say that there were not cases of abuse. Many slave owners took advantage of a law which permitted slaves to be substituted for their masters in the army. In total more than 3000 blacks would serve their new country, the majority of them doing so of their own free will. In point of fact approximately five percent of Washington's army at the time of the Battle of Monmouth was black. The average Continental battalion had 50 black soldiers. Washington was particularly proud of his black troops, several of whom were with him at the crossing of the Delaware before the Battle of Trenton. Although they were not normally segregated into their own units two all-black units did exist. One, a regiment from Rhode Island which never averaged more than 400 men, withstood a Hessian assault in which they were outnumbered three to one, repulsing the Hessians three separate times. It was a peculiar situation which might be difficult to appreciate, but although some states rewarded slaves who fought for the Revolution with their freedom, others returned to their former circumstance after the war.

Direct involvement in the war was not confined to the male population as women too played an important role. Although men did most of the actual fighting there are numerous accounts of women joining battle. Mary Hays manned a cannon in place of her fallen husband at the Battle of Monmouth. Molly Corbin took up her husband's musket when he fell in defense of Fort Washington. The whole concept of 'Molly Pitcher' described women who brought water and supplies to men on the battlefield. For the most part women were occupied in support of the armies. They cooked, nursed, sewed uniforms and did those things which were essential to keeping the vast armies functioning and moving. Revolutionary diary accounts praised the wives of men in the regiments for the comfort they brought to the harsh reality of war. However, women were also employed in more

dangerous capacities. Many were used as messengers between the armies and the government while others were used as spies to gather and transfer pertinent information. These examples illustrate the support that an ideal can evoke in determined, dedicated people regardless of race, creed, or sex and bind them into a fighting force which could challenge and overcome one of the strongest military powers of the time.

As the call to arms was made men, and women, of idealistic conviction became soldiers of the revolution. Initially they were volunteers, members of their states' militias which had been organized to augment the British Army in its protection of the colonies prior to 1775. The most disturbing problem encountered in the early days of conflict with Britain rose from the fact that militia were not bound to service. Troops would participate in skirmishes and battles near their homes then arbitrarily leave the ranks to fulfill personal commitments. There was also a problem convincing the militia to leave the borders of their own colony to continue engagements with the enemy.

The militia system was established to require able-bodied men between the ages of 16 and 50 years to report for service. As the colonial territories became more secure militia units in areas away from the

Right: A poster appealing for recruits for Washington's forces is combined with arms drill information.
Below: An American soldier of the War of Independence.

frontier became lax, developing a social club atmosphere. Officers were selected by ballot, the positions usually falling to men who were well liked or influential members of the community. Their military capabilities were rarely considered. This practice would be continued through the next century, though most military leaders realized the system was flawed. The most frequent complaint levied against the militia was its lack of discipline and unpredictability. Militia soldiers would fight well at times when even the toughest regular troops would have broken. At other times they routed at the least provocation. George Washington continually referred to these problems, explaining to the Continental Congress that if the colonies had any hope of winning the war that had begun they would have to consider raising and supporting a regular Continental Army.

In 1776 the Continental Congress acted on Washington's advice. Enlistments were changed requiring recruits to serve from one to three years or for the duration of the war in some instances. A bonus of 10 colonial dollars was given to a man for enlisting and basic army pay was approximately six dollars per month. Other incentives were added as the war years dragged on. Land was granted to veterans as payment for their years of service. Through the course of the war approximately 300,000 men served their new nation at one time or another, out of the total American population of three million. Some 17,000 men would actually be considered as regulars in the Continental Army. This army would form the nucleus of the future United States Army and although the Continentals never presented a uniform appearance nor equalled their British counterparts in equipment or materiel, they fought with a determination seldom seen on the battlefield. They were, in spite of their flaws and defects, able to win the war they had embarked upon.

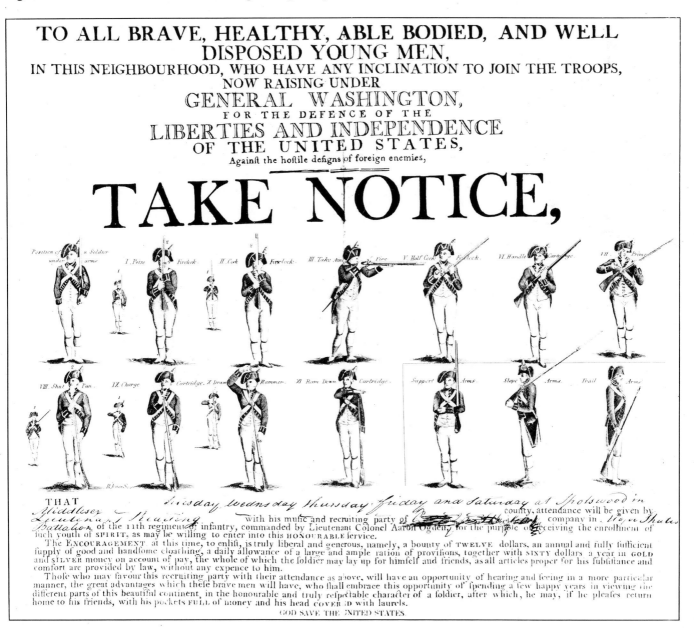

TO ALL BRAVE, HEALTHY, ABLE BODIED, AND WELL DISPOSED YOUNG MEN,
IN THIS NEIGHBOURHOOD, WHO HAVE ANY INCLINATION TO JOIN THE TROOPS, NOW RAISING UNDER
GENERAL WASHINGTON,
FOR THE DEFENCE OF THE
LIBERTIES AND INDEPENDENCE OF THE UNITED STATES,
Against the hostile designs of foreign enemies,

TAKE NOTICE,

5 THE SARATOGA CAMPAIGN

As the campaigns of 1776 drew to a close and the armies moved to winter quarters the British position was unsteady. The invasion from Canada by Sir Guy Carleton had failed without ever attaining its primary goals. Although the Americans took heavy losses with their flotilla force virtually destroyed Carleton's bid to capture Fort Ticonderoga had been compromised by General Howe's lack of support. Within two months Howe's New Jersey campaign had also collapsed after Washington's victories at Trenton and Princeton. The British position had reverted to its original stance, Carleton in Canada and Howe at New York. In an effort to alter the course of events by implementing his own strategy, General John Burgoyne, Carleton's second in command, took leave to return to England. There he presented his strategy to receptive Members of Parliament. Burgoyne believed that if the colonies could be split along the Lake Champlain-Hudson River line that the rebellion would be quelled. This would separate the more radical New

Englanders from the remaining colonies, thus isolating their influence over the more conservative faction.

Burgoyne's idea, documented in his, 'Thoughts for conducting the war from Canada' was not a new plan for this area. Carleton had laid out virtually the same strategy. The primary difference lay in the fact that Burgoyne envisioned the campaign as part of a three-pronged offensive. He saw Carleton's failure as a direct result of insufficient support and political backing from Britain. Burgoyne's strategy was to launch the main attack along the water highway of the Lake Champlain-Hudson River Valley, driving to New York's capital at Albany. Two supporting offensives would be staged; one through the Mohawk

Right: A group of British and Hessian soldiers. On campaign few would have been able to keep uniforms as neat as those shown here.
Far left: General John 'Gentleman Johnny' Burgoyne from the painting by Joshua Reynolds.
Below: Burgoyne talks with a group of Indian leaders. The use of Indians by the British helped recruiting for the American forces because of fear of Indian attacks.

Valley west of Albany and the other along the Hudson River from the south. Burgoyne used his political influence to champion his scheme. The Secretary of State responsible for the Americas Lord George Germain and King George believed that Burgoyne's strategy was perfect, agreeing that this enterprising officer was the man they needed to put new spirit into the British forces in the colonies. Although Burgoyne was not interested in the overall command he continued a fierce lobby for his grand strategy.

Burgoyne made certain that Carleton remained as the Governor of Canada in spite of the fact that Germain wanted Burgoyne to fill that position. Burgoyne did not want the added responsibility of the governorship, merely wanting Carleton to be given

instructions to provide logistical support for Burgoyne's operation and not attempt to interfere in the mechanics of the strategy.

Burgoyne's optimism spread to the government and they became convinced that the execution of his plans would bring the war to an end within the year. They approved the strategy, giving Burgoyne a free rein to implement it but then destroyed all its chances of success. Howe applied for and was given permission to launch a campaign against Philadelphia at the same time Burgoyne would be making his advance toward Albany. Although General Clinton, Howe's second in command, argued that the campaign should not begin until Burgoyne's offensive was assured of victory, Howe refused to cooperate. Clinton realized that Washington's army around Philadelphia would never move from that area and that the troops that Howe wanted to use in a campaign against Philadelphia would be of much greater value in the effort to subdue New York state. The Philadelphia garrison would still be there when the troops returned from their mission with Burgoyne. However, Howe believed in the long-accepted principle that once a nation's capital was taken that nation would soon capitulate or collapse. He also believed that he could trap and capture the rebellion's leaders in their capital. What he apparently failed to realize was that the American capital was newly established and that if Philadelphia was endangered the Continental Congress would simply move to another city proclaiming it their new capital. Howe had official approval for his campaign and would not be dissuaded. He set about formulating his battle plans and assigning troops for the assault. He would not openly defy his orders to support Burgoyne but that support would be a token gesture as he had not been given orders laying down to what degree he was to support the Albany venture. He

41

placed Clinton in command of a weak corps, which would have little offensive potential, and sent it to a position along the line to Albany. Had it not been for the government's inability to formulate an encompassing strategy for the war effort or the rift between Howe and Burgoyne, the invasion from Canada coupled with a later assault on Philadelphia might well have forced the colonies to capitulate.

By 21 June 1777 Burgoyne's army was prepared to leave Canada. His initial plans had called for the invasion to begin one month earlier but logistic problems and the positioning of troops under the command of Lieutenant Colonel Barry St Leger, delayed him. St Leger, with a force composed largely of Tory troops and Indians, was sailing from Montreal along the St Lawrence to Lake Ontario to land at Oswego for an attack on the American Fort Stanwix. After that mission was accomplished St Leger was to proceed down the Mohawk Valley to Albany. Burgoyne's logistic difficulties were monumental. His army consisted of approximately 10,000 troops with seven British regiments, five Hessian regiments and assorted units of Loyalists, Indians and Canadian volunteers. Burgoyne put great faith in the ability of those latter units to provide excellent scouting and as foraging parties to supply food for the army. He had also assembled no fewer than 138 artillery pieces, which would prove to be the largest artillery train collected for any one operation in the entire war. Even by European standards it was an immense artillery force for an army of this size and it would be very difficult to move through the dense wilderness of upper New York.

Within a few days of leaving St Johns Burgoyne realized that his army was overburdened by the accompanying entourage he had collected. A primary example of the extent of Burgoyne's 'necessities' was the accompanying three wagons-full of the general's personal gear. Movement through the wilderness was at a snail's pace. Another problem which soon became apparent was that created by the 400 Indians who accompanied the army. They could not be kept disciplined beyond the boundaries of the army's camp. One of Burgoyne's officers later wrote that the Indians and the white men who helped maintain them behaved like spoiled children, refusing to do anything but what they wished.

The Americans had little to oppose Burgoyne in that area. The first objective was Fort Ticonderoga. This fortification had fallen into a deplorable state during the year that the Americans occupied it. Major General Arthur St Clair commanded the fort, which was by that time little more than a pile of tumbled logs. The only defensible positions were on the earthen mounds which the French had built many years earlier. St Clair's force of 2000 men had been reduced by sickness to an able-bodied garrison of approximately 500. The harsh winter and illness had caused morale

Left: General Horatio Gates who commanded the American forces in the later stages of the Saratoga Campaign.
Right: American soldiers on the look out for Indians move through difficult forest country.
Below: Hessian soldiers accompanied by camp followers on the march. Such hangers-on helped slow Burgoyne's advance.

and discipline to deteriorate. Fort Ticonderoga was of strategic importance to the defense of New York from northern invasion as it was actually the only major fortification between Canada and Albany. Therefore its deplorable condition was critical. Also defending the colony was the Army of the Northern Department, approximately the same size as St Clair's force. This unit was camped 40 miles south of Fort Ticonderoga at Fort Edwards. Although known as a fort it was actually nothing more than a staging area for the army. The Army of the Northern Department was commanded by Major General Philip Schuyler, who met prejudice throughout his service as many believed him a Tory sympathizer.

Politics played as important a role within the American command as it had for the British. Schuyler's predecessor and chief rival for command of the army was Major General Horatio Gates. Gates persistently brought charges against Schuyler before the Continental Congress, which eventually resulted in his assumption of Schuyler's command. Gates used

Schuyler's pessimistic view of the situation in New York against him, though in fact Schuyler had just cause for his sentiments. The Army of the Northern Department was poorly armed and equipped. The men were poorly clothed, suffering from various ailments and a decline in morale which made them no match for a concerted British effort in their area. This did not mean, however, that Schuyler was neglecting his duties, only that he recognized the gravity of the situation. Schuyler promised to do the best he could while Gates promised victory if given the command.

By 2 July the British army had reached the outer defenses of Fort Ticonderoga. St Clair recognized that the situation on his perimeter was hopeless and withdrew to the old French lines to make a stand. It was not a bad plan as St Clair knew that in 1758 the French had taken a similar position and had given the British a sound defeat. Burgoyne realized that the French fortification line would be difficult to crack but he did not intend to make the same mistakes as his predecessors. Major General William Phillips, Burgoyne's second in command who also commanded the British artillery, proposed that the weakness of the fortification lay in the fact that the colonists had neglected to fortify Mount Defiance just south of the fortress. From this hill British artillery would have a full field of fire over not only the fortification but Lake Champlain itself. On Burgoyne's orders Phillips sent a small reconnaissance party to Mount Defiance.

Upon their return the officer in charge reported that the only path to the top of the hill was better suited to goats than men, to say nothing of artillery. In reply Phillips claimed that where a goat could go a man could go, and where a man could go he could drag a gun.

For the following three days Phillips' artillerymen cut a crude path up Mount Defiance and by 5 July had pulled two artillery pieces to the summit. Phillips' feat meant the destruction of Fort Ticonderoga and the smaller defensive position at nearby Fort Independence. St Clair had no option but to attempt to evacuate his garrison. That night his force crossed the pontoon bridge that linked the two fortifications, beginning a retreat toward Vermont. The bulk of the force moved toward Castleton, Vermont while the more able-bodied of his command set up a rear guard under the leadership of Colonel Francis. Although St Clair accomplished his evacuation his retreat did not go unnoticed. By morning Burgyone had sent Brigadier General Simon Fraser's advance guard of grenadiers, light infantry of the 24th Regiment and elements of the Tory units in pursuit of the Americans. General von Riedesel's Hessian brigade followed slowly behind Fraser.

On 7 July Fraser's troops engaged Francis' rear guard in a brisk battle at Hubbardton. Initially a large proportion of the American force fled on contact with the British but Colonel Seth Warner's Green Mountain Boys broke the first British assault with several accurate volleys. They then counterattacked, catching the British completely off guard. The counterattack threatened to rout the British from the field but von Riedesel's brigade arrived to stabilize their position. With von Riedesel's support the British renewed their assault. Francis was killed and his force suffered some 360 casualties but Fraser failed to follow through with his attack and the main American force was able to escape. Five days later St Clair joined Schuyler at Fort Edwards.

During this time Burgoyne met and destroyed an American flotilla which stood in his path at Skenesboro. The road was now open for the army to march on Fort Edwards and from there to Albany. However, rather than turn back to the immediate line of advance along the Hudson River as planned, Burgoyne decided to take a course through 23 miles of wilderness. This one decision to vary his original strategy cost Burgoyne the entire campaign. That 23 mile march would take 24 days to accomplish. Although there are no true records of the reasons for his change in strategy there is evidence that a desire for personal gain overrode sound military judgement. Apparently Major Philip Skene, Burgoyne's chief Tory aide, convinced the General that the venture would be successful. Skene allegedly had a 25,000 acre land grant in this area and by convincing Burgoyne to drive through the wilderness a road would be built, thus increasing Skene's potential profits on the land.

No other reason has ever been provided to account for Burgoyne's decision.

The road which the British army had to build was no less than 23 miles long with four bridges and a two mile causeway. As the British worked Schuyler did not remain inactive. He made every effort to hamper the British advance, detaching units of frontiersmen to harass the troops and invoking a scorched earth policy to deny the British the opportunity to forage. He also intersected the road whenever possible to slow Burgoyne's supply train. Nevertheless Schuyler was having difficulties of his own. The loss of Fort Ticonderoga had caused a serious morale problem. Colonial settlers in the area were in a state of panic, primarily because Burgoyne was known to be employing Indians. Many feared that Burgoyne would simply loose the Indians and that the American forces would be unable to protect them. This fear would later prove to be Burgoyne's final undoing as colonists throughout the New York and Vermont region rallied against him after the murder of a young woman, Jane McCrea. This senseless killing united all the settlers, including those who had previously remained neutral, and brought a sizeable force to bear on Burgoyne.

Schuyler also had to contend with the problem of enlistment expirations. With the balance apparently against them the volunteers were not likely to remain beyond their enlistment dates. Two Massachusetts regiments marched away from Fort Edwards when their service obligations expired and there was nothing Schuyler could do to stop them. Just when it appeared that the entire Northern Department was on the verge of collapse the situation began to change. St Leger's Tory-Indian force had reached Fort Stanwix only to discover that the American troops in that sector were ready and able to fight. St Leger expected the fortification to fall easily but the 750-man garrison commanded by Colonel Peter Gansevoort had prepared its defenses well and offered staunch resistance. St Leger was forced to lay siege to the fort. While he was halted outside the garrison General Nicholas Herkimer raised a force of militia and Indians in Tryon County and marched to raise the siege. On 6 August his 800 men blundered into an ambush laid by St Leger. Herkimer was killed in the battle but the militia inflicted sufficient casualties on the Tory force that St Leger had to withdraw from the engagement. The militia success at the Battle of Oriskany jeopardized St Leger's position at Fort Stanwix. On 22 August he learned that General Benedict Arnold was advancing with a relief column of Continental regulars. This information broke the morale of St Leger's Indian units and he had insufficient Tory units to stand against a concerted American assault. He retreated to Oswego.

St Leger's retreat was the spark needed to bring the American armies in the area back to life. This

Above: General Benedict
Arnold played an important role
in the final battles of the
Saratoga Campaign.
Left: The British generals are
portrayed as paying for the
taking of scalps.
Below: A scene from the Battle
of Oriskany, fought on
6 August 1777, an important
success for the American forces.

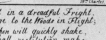

condition was further enhanced when during that
same time a force of 800 Hessian and Tory troops
commanded by Lieutenant Colonel Frederick Baum
was thwarted in an attempt to capture an arsenal at
Bennington, Vermont. During the march to Bennington the force was persistently harassed by American
riflemen. On 14 August a skirmish was fought with
the American troops of Colonel John Stark. Although
Baum's Hessians drove the Americans off, he recalled
his men when more militia were spotted outside
Bennington. To make matters worse for Burgoyne his
Indians were living up to the expectations and fears
of the colonists and their activities brought more men
to the American ranks.

On 15 August Burgoyne sent a relief column of 550
men toward Bennington. The following day Stark
ordered a full assault, declaring that the Americans
would 'either win the battle today' or his 'wife would
be a widow by nightfall.' Warner's Green Mountain
Boys had joined Stark's force and once again their
deadly accuracy inflicted devastating casualties.
Stark's attack cost him 70 men but the two Hessian
columns had 270 killed and more than 700 captured.
The battle at Bennington destroyed any illusions
which existed of the inability of colonial militia to
defeat British and Hessian regulars.

Supplies for the growing army continued to be a
problem, but the morale of the American forces was
at its highest peak. On 19 August General Gates took
command of the Department. Under him were two
of the finest officers in the Continental Army at that
time, Colonel Daniel Morgan and General Benedict
Arnold. Burgoyne was faced with only two options,
to push on or retreat from the area entirely. He chose
to advance. This was not as foolish as it might appear
as Burgoyne was under the impression that Howe was
advancing south of the American army. By continuing
to advance Burgoyne believed that he and Howe would
trap the Americans between them. On 13 September
Burgoyne crossed to the west bank of the Hudson
River where he encountered a force of more than 9000
American troops entrenched in a strong position on
Bemis Heights. Those heights blocked the road to
Albany, forcing Burgoyne to halt. After considering
his options Burgoyne attacked on 19 September. His
assault was directed at the left flank in an attempt to
gain a position on the high ground quickly. The
Americans were prepared for such an attack, stopping
Burgoyne's forces far short of their objective. Burgoyne refused to concede defeat. All through that day
he threw units into the attack hoping to breach the
defenses by sheer weight of numbers. By 1400 hours
the Americans had launched six major counter-
attacks, driving the British back only then to be halted
themselves. For three more hours the battle swayed
back and forth. At 1700 hours, despite heavy casualties, Burgoyne ordered another assault which
succeeded in forcing the Americans back.

The battle had thus far cost Burgoyne 600 men, twice the number of American casualties, but he considered it a victory preparing to renew the assault on the following day. Burgoyne's plans could not be executed. Fraser informed him that the men were exhausted and their casualties too high to permit assaults on the following day. Almost simultaneously Burgoyne learned that Clinton's forces were moving north to rendezvous with him. He decided the best strategy for the moment would be to dig in and await Clinton's arrival. For three weeks Burgoyne waited in vain. Though Clinton moved north along the Hudson and had by October succeeded in capturing several smaller fortifications south of Albany, he had neither the men nor the materiel to continue his advance. Fearing the destruction of his small corps Clinton halted momentarily then returned to the protection of the city of New York.

Burgoyne was forced to face the realities of his situation. Against the advice of his senior officers he ordered a final assault on the American positions. He had only 6000 men with which to challenge Gates' 11,000 on the heights. At 1100 hours on 7 October Burgoyne led the final attack of his Saratoga Campaign. American pickets sounded the alarm and Gates' adjutant-general, Lieutenant Colonel James Wilkinson, moved forward to investigate the British positions noticing a weakness in the British right flank. Gates responded by sending Morgan's riflemen opposite that flank. Benedict Arnold, who had been removed from command after a quarrel with Gates, heard the sound of gunfire and rushed from his camp. On the line he assumed command of his men in spite of Gates' orders. The initial American volleys shattered the British lines, but General Fraser was able to form a new line with the 24th Regiment. Arnold immediately led a brigade of more than 3000 New York militia against von Riedesel's Hessian troops. The British and Hessians were outnumbered almost six to one on this flank and their lines disintegrated. One of Morgan's legendary Indian fighters, Tim Murphy, added the final blow when he shot and killed General Fraser. With Fraser dead and the right flank routed, Arnold capitalized on the situation by leading attacks against the British reserves. During the attack Arnold received a serious wound, of which he nearly died, but he refused to leave the field until the action was over.

By the evening of that day the American forces were victorious. Burgoyne had more than 600 casualties, including many officers, while the Americans had suffered only 200 losses. On the night of 8 October during a severe storm Burgoyne began an eight mile retreat to Saratoga. There he hoped to use the river to return to Canada, but the Americans had anticipated that possibility. Artillery had been positioned along Burgoyne's avenue of retreat. Reconnaissance of the area proved that his position was hopeless. Although his army had been augmented by units which had guarded his lines of communication and supply, his force numbered only 5500 against a suspected American force of more than 20,000. On 17 October he surrendered his entire command to General Gates.

The most important aspect of the campaign was the ability of the American armies to convert early defeat into victory. The American Revolution had gained respectability during those months. European nations, primarily France, responded to the Saratoga success by openly declaring a treaty of mutual aid and commerce. The alliance would mean troops, supplies and the support of the French fleet, but most importantly it legitimized the course set by the colonies and recognized them as an entity independent of Britain. The American armies would suffer setbacks in the years ahead, but the events of those first 15 months of the Revolution had proven that the Continental Army, the militia and the military leaders of the United States of America were able to face up to the British Army.

6 THE WAR IN THE NORTH

The year 1777 saw not only the start of Burgoyne's campaign to 'win the war' but another equally important campaign by General Howe against the American capital, Philadelphia. Despite the fact that he had promised the government in London that he would support Burgoyne's venture, Howe had his own ideas on the strategic objectives necessary for victory. He considered the capture of an enemy's capital tantamount to victory, failing to recognize that Philadelphia was as yet only a center for conducting the business of the Continental Congress, not the heart of the American states.

Howe considered two possibilities for his effort to capture the city. He could move across New Jersey and then cross the Delaware River to put a force north of the city and assault from there. He realized that Washington would have to position his army between the city and the British army. At some point during the campaign Howe would engage Washington in a pitched battle. He was certain that he would then destroy the American army once and for all. The alternate plan involved transporting his entire army by water, then moving either on the Chesapeake or Delaware to land south of Philadelphia. This was an extremely hazardous route, yet if successful would be the more effective strategy. As he considered his options Howe contented himself with conducting raids in the surrounding area of New Jersey and Connecticut. However, his procrastination once spring arrived gave Washington valuable time to reorganize his army. The winter at Morristown had been harsh but with the spring enlistments swelled

Washington's ranks and the army regained its strength.

In June 1777 Howe became more aggressive, maneuvering his forces against Washington's defenses in the Watchung Mountains. This operation produced few results. Later that month Howe attempted to draw Washington into the open by feigning a retreat, but Washington was not fooled. Finally at the end of June Howe decided to take his army via the water route to the south of Philadelphia. As Burgoyne's army was at that same time beginning its operations in northern New York Howe hoped that troops would be drawn away from Washington's army to reinforce Ticonderoga. On 23 July the British fleet sailed from Sandyhook, New Jersey. In less than one week they were positioned at the mouth of the Delaware River. There Howe had to alter his plans in response to reports that the Americans had constructed obstacles to protect this region from an amphibious assault. Howe changed course and maneuvered toward the Chesapeake.

Howe's sea maneuvers were causing Washington difficulty because he had been prepared for a land invasion across New Jersey. It was not until 22 August that the American leaders realized that Howe was going to use the Chesapeake Bay route, which forced Washington to move quickly to protect Philadelphia from the south. On 25 August Howe landed at Elkton, Maryland, approximately 50 miles southwest of Philadelphia. Washington, with 11,000 men, took a position on the eastern side of Brandywine Creek. There he and Generals Greene and Sullivan waited for Howe's 18,000-strong army. Howe attacked on 11 September, using the same flanking maneuvers he employed at the battles in New York. The American army held until a move by General Cornwallis against the right flank threw the entire Continental Army into full retreat. Although for the most part the American units withdrew in good order the battle was costly with approximately 500 casualties.

Washington maneuvered his army toward Chester, Pennsylvania, some 10 miles southwest of Philadelphia. For two weeks he stood his ground to prevent Howe from entering the city but finally Howe gained the upper hand. Washington had been maneuvered into a position where an effort to continue to protect the capital could mean the complete destruction of his army. He therefore decided to move to a position across the Schuylkill River and on 26 September Cornwallis' forces marched into Philadelphia unopposed. The army was greeted with enthusiasm by the Tory population of the city. The Revolutionary leaders had fled to Lancaster, Pennsylvania. The capture of Philadelphia, the second largest city in the English-speaking world, was indeed a prize. Most importantly it gave reassurance to Parliament that the British Army could bring the colonies back into line. Militarily it meant nothing, which Howe was forced to admit. True success lay in the defeat of Washington's army.

Howe established his headquarters six miles north of Philadelphia at a small settlement called Germantown where he placed a 9000 man contingent. He ordered strong patrolling of the area but made no effort to construct fortifications except for one small redoubt. The laying of defenses would have been an admission that Washington could strike again and that he feared such an assault. Howe was confident that Washington would not dare to attack so large a force of British regulars. He was wrong. Washington was

Right: A poster calling for recruits for a loyalist unit.
Below: Washington and a group of his senior officers with the army in winter quarters at Valley Forge.

Above: Baron von Steuben.
Right: Steuben instructs
recruits at Valley Forge.

preparing a surprise attack which if successful would not only inflict heavy casualties on the British but would put Howe in a compromised position, forcing him to withdraw. Philadelphia would then be retaken by the Americans.

Washington's attack was based on a series of complex maneuvers, requiring precise coordination. Under cover of dense fog on 4 October he began his attack by striking the British center with two large columns while two other columns simultaneously attacked both British flanks. The assault was initially successful but as the day wore on the British offered stiff resistance at Chew House. Coordination between the columns was lost and the attack lost momentum. However, the battle was still going in Washington's favor until disaster struck. In the confusion several American regiments became disoriented and opened fire on one another in the belief that they had contacted the enemy. With the exchange of volleys rumors began to spread through the army that the British had maneuvered to their rear. Panic engulfed the army and neither Washington nor his officers could restore order. A disorderly retreat bordering on rout resulted.

The battle had cost Washington dearly as American killed and wounded were estimated at 700 with approximately 400 more missing or captured. Howe made an official statement that his casualties were under 500, though officers present at the battle would later confess that the total had been above 800. Strangely, despite the losses at Brandywine and Germantown and the occupation of the American capital, morale in Washington's army remained high. In December he took his army to winter quarters at a site known as Valley Forge. Although the year's end had brought news of Gates' victory in upper New York and the alliance with France, Washington knew that the true test of his army's resolve would come during the winter months. He could not tolerate the slow disintegration of his forces during the winter and

would repeatedly complain that winter quartering was more costly than any battle.

Washington selected Valley Forge for two main reasons. First he wanted to continue to protect Pennsylvania and New Jersey from Tory raids which might be mounted in that area. Second, from that position he could guard the main road which ran from the south to New England. Unfortunately the area around Valley Forge was desolate because it had been ravaged by the first year of war. Most supplies had been exhausted and the local population had barely enough food for themselves with nothing to spare for Washington's troops. Although his reasoning was sound he was criticized for attempting to accomplish too much and in so doing placing the army in jeopardy. Washington would discover that not only was the local population unable to help him but the Continental Congress and the quartermasters would fail to secure even the most meager supplies for his troops. As time went on and supplies from other colonies became available, arguments over the sale and distribution of those supplies kept them from reaching Valley Forge. In some areas, such as Boston, merchants would deal with the Continental Army or Congress only when large inflated profits could be made, refusing to accept Continental scrip as payment for their goods.

Washington was forced to watch as more than 2500 of his men died of starvation and exposure. Another 2000 refused to extend their enlistments or deserted. By the end of winter his army had been reduced to fewer than 6000 men, half of whom were unfit for duty. He did not receive relief from the Pennsylvania Legislature which turned a deaf ear to his requests, concerning themselves with sanctions against him for failing to mount attacks against the British forces comfortably housed in Philadelphia.

In spite of the adversities one important accomplishment was made at Valley Forge. A former Prussian officer, Baron von Steuben, arrived on the scene. This staunch professional old soldier was given the rank of general and began an extensive training program. Although he spoke little English he carefully transcribed a routine of drill and discipline for the army. His drills were based on a simplified version of European and British training programs. His execution of the instruction was brilliant. He began with a small unit of 120 men, taking complete charge and guiding them as a schoolmaster would children. By the time he had completed his instruction each man had mastered the system. The unit was then broken up and the men returned to their former units where they then became the instructors. The results were astonishing. In less than one month the army, primarily those known as the regulars, had mastered the drills and performed maneuvers never before believed possible. All aspects of military discipline, including the proper use of the bayonet as a weapon rather than a cooking utensil, were conveyed.

By March 1778 the army was no longer a rag-tag of militia but an organization of professional soldiers. Training continued throughout April and the early weeks of May as von Steuben transformed the army into a disciplined fighting machine. Military men such as Brigadier General Marquis de Lafayette would be moved to state that Washington's Continental Army was actually 'more dangerous than the British Army or any other European army in existence.' General von Steuben had accomplished the seemingly impossible and on their next encounter the British would discover that the Americans had matured into a force which was more than equal to their own.

The winter of 1777–78 would be the undoing of the British. Howe ignored an excellent opportunity to destroy Washington at Valley Forge. Had he struck during the early months of winter Washington would have been defeated, off-setting the failure of Burgoyne's Saratoga Campaign. As a result of Howe's apparent indecisiveness the government dismissed him, placing General Clinton in his stead.

In accordance with his orders to reconsolidate the British war effort Clinton moved his army from Philadelphia to New York in early June 1778. This maneuver surprised Washington but he took advantage of the situation by sending a contingent under General Charles Lee to strike at Clinton's extended lines on the march to New York. Lee attacked the British rear guard on 28 June near Monmouth Courthouse. Clinton reacted immediately sending his nearest division to aid and protect his army's rear. At this point the American contingent fell into chaos. Generals 'Mad' Anthony Wayne, Charles Scott and Lafayette became confused by the orders given them by Lee and before the situation could be resolved the American attack collapsed. The British counter-attacked forcing the Americans to retreat.

Lee's mismanagement of the affair caused Washington to take matters into his own hands. He rode directly to the front, rallied his troops and established a temporary defensive line. He then reprimanded Lee and removed him from command. Clinton, encouraged by the rout, led his troops against the forming American defense but was surprised when his assault was abruptly halted. He then attempted a flanking maneuver which was repulsed and after being thrown back on three separate occasions by Wayne's troops, Clinton decided to disengage.

Although Washington ordered a counterattack his troops were not fit to execute it. After traveling less than 100 yards the assault faltered and dissolved. The Battle of Monmouth was over. Clinton moved away, installing himself in New York City shortly thereafter. Washington followed, taking a position at White Plains in a bid to counter Clinton's next move.

Monmouth was the last major battle in the north between the two armies. From that time on the war in the north would be primarily one of raids and counter-raids. One of the most noted of these operations occurred on 3–4 July 1778. A Tory force of approximately 1100 men attacked a garrison of Patriots near what is now Wilkes-Barre, Pennsylvania. The incident would have been little more than a minor defeat had not the Tory Rangers and Indians involved in the raid committed what became known as the Wyoming Massacre. Hatred between Tory and Patriot factions had become intense and in an expression of that hatred the garrison was brutally murdered after their defeat. The majority of prisoners taken were burned alive, held in a fire by pitchfork-wielding Tory troops. Also during the Massacre 227 scalps were taken, most of them by what the Americans would refer to as 'His Majesty's blue-eyed Indians.' Incidents such as this sparked a rash of senseless bloodshed which complicated the war and converted minor engagements into vengeful reprisals. The Wyoming Massacre also had far-reaching consequences with regard to Indian relations. In response to the role played by the Indians Washington vented his wrath on the Six Nations of the Iroquois. In August 1778 he sent a force under the command of General Sullivan against the Iroquois. Sullivan's successful operation literally destroyed the Iroquois as a fighting force.

Other actions during this time included an expedition by Colonel George Rogers Clark into the northwest region claimed as part of the Virginia Colony. With a small contingent of frontiersmen and Indians Clark captured the British forts at Kaskaskia, Cahokia and Vincennes. However, in December 1778 he would suffer a setback when the British recaptured Vincennes but by February 1779 he defeated that garrison and reclaimed the fortification. His success put the Northwest Territory once and for all in the hands of the Americans.

Another important incident occurred in 1780 when Major General Benedict Arnold attempted to surrender West Point to the British through contact with a British spy, Major John Andre. The conspiracy lasted 16 months, failing after Andre was captured by Patriot forces. In October Arnold escaped capture to spend the remainder of the war in British service. Arnold's actions were a severe shock to all as he had repeatedly demonstrated his military skills and bravery on behalf of the Revolution. His only defense rests in the fact that he had consistently been overlooked for promotions and commands, which went to less qualified officers with more powerful political connections. He lost faith in the principles and ideals for which he had fought so well. Another influential factor was his 1779 marriage to Peggy Shippen whose family had strong Tory ties. Caught between her extravagant tastes and persistent nagging and his own disillusion with the war Arnold embarked on a course which made him America's most despised traitor when he should have been a noted hero.

The armies in the north remained in deadlock and so attention shifted to the south as Britain made its final bid to regain control of its American colonies.

Right: The Marquis de Lafayette by Charles Wilson Peale.
Below: The British garrison of Vincennes surrenders, 1779.

7 THE WAR AT SEA

At the outbreak of war the New England colonies had a minimal sea force made up of small vessels of the sloop or schooner types. Such ships were armed primarily for defense, many of them being smuggling vessels. When the war began the colonial leaders soon realized that pressure would have to be brought against Britain's sea lanes if the colonies were to have any hope of bringing the war to a swift conclusion. Washington took a strong position on this issue, urging Congress to begin programs to provide for a colonial navy.

The need was obvious. Perhaps most importantly a colonial naval force could disrupt British shipping, inhibiting the transfer of men and materiel which Britain needed to fight the war. Secondly, as ships captured during time of war could have their cargoes confiscated, the seizure of such goods would provide supplies and revenue for the Continental Congress and Army. In spite of these points the Congress was slow to act, being initially more concerned with political matters than the war. The responsibility for creating a naval force fell to George Washington. He in turn relied on the abilities of a Marblehead fisherman, John Manley, who took command of six schooners and one brigantine as the initial ocean fleet of 1775. In the fall of that same year the Congress voted to build five warships and refit three other merchant vessels as warships. This fleet was to be placed under the command of Commodore Hopkins with the objective of attacking the Bahamas in February 1776. Hopkins' initial venture was successful in that it captured more than 100 cannon, two British frigates and the governor of the Bahamas himself. However, on its return voyage the fleet was blockaded at Newport, Rhode Island, when it attempted to land after an epidemic of small-pox broke out among its sailors.

In June 1776 the colonial vessel *Andrew Dorea* captured two British transports loaded with troops and in August John Paul Jones in his ship *The Providence* raided Nova Scotia, capturing no fewer than 16 vessels and their cargoes by October. In spite of the many successes in the early months of the war, the naval aspects of the war were largely confined to the accomplishments of privateers. It has been estimated that some 2000 vessels were commissioned by the Continental Congress at one time or another as

privateers. During the eight years of war those vessels captured approximately 600 British ships and confiscated $18,000,000 worth of property. The most famous privateer, the *Rattlesnake*, captured cargoes worth more than $1,000,000 in one cruise in the Baltic.

Although the figures listed for the success of privateers are astounding, and illustrate Washington's theory that America could support its war effort through the capture and sale of ships and cargo, little of the money received was ever placed in the treasury of the Continental Congress. When ships and their cargo were sold in foreign ports the officers and crews of the privateers usually divided the profits among themselves as just reward for their efforts. The war they waged at sea was a great nuisance to Britain and did much to raise the morale of colonial land forces, but it did little to promote the overall war effort.

The navy's most influential supporter was Benjamin Franklin, who increased the naval capabilities of the colonies when he signed an alliance treaty with France in 1778. France had a fleet equal to that of the British fleet being employed against the colonies. Spain, allied to France, was also drawn into the conflict,

Above: Benjamin Franklin
aboard the *Repulse* on the way to
France to negotiate the
alliance and naval assistance.
Left: Commodore Esek
Hopkins, first Commander in
Chief of the American Fleet.
Right: A French engraving of
the Battle of Chesapeake Bay
(also known as the Virginia
Capes) in which a British
attempt to break the blockade
of Yorktown was defeated by
the French under de Grasse.

Left: John Paul Jones refuses the surrender demand from the *Serapis*. Jones' leadership was the deciding factor in the battle.
Far left: Despite the successes achieved by the ships under Jones' command and his reputation as the founder of the American Navy and as the most dashing of its early leaders, Jones received little employment after his victory over the *Serapis* and after working in Russia he died in Paris in 1792.
Below: An impression of the battle between the *Bon Homme Richard* and the *Serapis*. The British ship gained the upper hand in the gunnery duel but Jones won the battle by a boarding attack.

swinging the balance of naval power firmly in favor of the Americans. Together France and Spain had 90 ships-of-the-line, first class warships, as compared to the 72 possessed by Britain. Franklin was also promised several 30-gun frigates by the French, which helped solve the colonial problem of building a naval force. French and Spanish ports became safe havens for the American navy and privateers.

The most famous naval figure to emerge from the Revolution was John Paul Jones. His career, though brief, was the foundation on which naval tradition in America was laid. Jones' first command was of an 18-gun sloop, *Ranger*, which sailed from the colonies in November 1777. In one month he returned with two captured vessels. In February 1778 he received the first salute ever given to an American vessel by a foreign ship, the French *Robuste*. During that same

year Jones cruised in the Irish Sea where he captured the first British warship to be taken during the Revolution, HMS *Drake*, which he set fire to at Whitehaven. In 1779 the French gave Jones an old East Indiaman the *Duc-de-Duras*. Jones renamed the vessel in honor of his friend Benjamin Franklin's book *Poor Richard's Almanac* but it became most widely known as the *Bon Homme Richard*. Jones oversaw the refitting of the *Bon Homme Richard* with six 18-pound cannon mounted on the lower deck, twenty-eight 12-pound cannon on the upper deck and eight 9-pound cannon fore and aft. The crew was comprised of a mixture of several nationalities, who fought more for the profits to be made in privateering than for the cause of the Revolution.

The *Bon Homme Richard* sailed with a small squadron of French vessels and although several

55

captures were made, inclement weather and lack of cooperation between the French captains and Jones led to confusion and hostility. Nonetheless on 23 September 1779 Jones fought the battle which set the standards of American naval tradition. Jones' squadron encountered a small British convoy escorted by warships. One of those vessels was the 44-gun frigate, HMS *Serapis*, commanded by Captain Richard Pearson, another the 20-gun brigantine the *Countess of Scarborough*. Jones' *Bon Homme Richard* joined battle primarily with the *Serapis* and he received no support from the French commander throughout the entire engagement. Before long Jones' ship, which had been out-maneuvered and was certainly outgunned, was badly damaged. All of his 12- and 18-pound guns were unable to fire and only three of his 9-pounders were serviceable. Many members of his crew called upon Jones to strike the colors and surrender, as did the captain of the *Serapis*. To Pearson's demand that he strike Jones immediately replied that he would rather sink first and issued his much misquoted response, 'I haven't begun to fight yet.' Those were rash words from a man who was fighting so powerful a British warship unaided and was in danger of having his ship literally shot from beneath him. With his vessel taking in water Jones realized that his only chance lay in grappling with the *Serapis*. After two attempts the ships were lashed together and Jones and 40 of his men boarded the British vessel. Jones had almost succeeded in capturing the ship when the French ship the *Alliance* moved forward to fire on the helpless *Serapis*. Pearson struck his colors. Once all his crew were safely aboard the captured ship Jones cut the vessels free and the *Bon Homme Richard* sank.

After so glorious a victory Jones sailed the *Serapis* to Brest but was never offered another commission in the American navy. Instead, with permission from Congress he accepted a commission from Catherine the Great to help organize and build the Russian Navy in the Black Sea. John Paul Jones died in Paris in 1792, virtually forgotten by the majority of Americans. He had served the United States with pride and distinction, being the only naval commander who was neither courtmartialled nor brought up on charges for profiteering. His country never rewarded him during his lifetime, but after his death his exploits would be publicized and romanticized as an example of one man's contribution to the cause of freedom.

From 1779–81 the French fleets would be principally responsible for the American naval war. One American venture off the coast of Maine in 1779 ended in disaster when the British trapped an entire fleet of seven Continental warships, 12 privateers, and 22 transports. All the vessels were burned and more than 500 sailors were captured. In 1781 a French fleet commanded by Admiral de Grasse left

Above: Captain Richard Pearson commanded the *Serapis* during the engagement with the *Bon Homme Richard*.

the French port at Brest bound for the West Indies. That fleet was diverted and from 5–9 September engaged Admiral Graves' British fleet at Chesapeake Bay. The battle ended only after Graves successfully outmaneuvered de Grasse and returned to New York. In so doing Graves left General Cornwallis to his fate at Yorktown.

The French were not the only nation to aid the American naval effort during this time. European nations had long resented the interference of the British with neutral shipping. Those nations, including Russia, Sweden, Denmark, Prussia, Portugal and Naples formed the League of Armed Neutrals, arming their ships to oppose British actions on the high seas. It was therefore a combined effort between European nations, American warships and privateers which put such a heavy burden on British shipping after 1779 that the British merchants lobbied for peace to achieve economic stability once again.

The full ramifications of war at sea had been something for which Britain was not prepared, and although the American role was small, standards were set which would be reflected in the traditions of the United States Navy.

8 THE WORLD TURNED UPSIDE-DOWN

In 1778 Britain embarked on a new strategy to salvage its war effort in the Americas. The disastrous, unproductive campaigns in the north convinced the government that it was likely that the war could not be won by fighting in the north. Attention was focussed on objectives in the southern colonies where a stronger Loyalist community was to be found. The war had become one of attrition and if Britain could exert control over the south the radical New Englanders would be forced to reconsider their position.

The first phase of the new strategy began when General Clinton sent a force of 3500 men under Lieutenant Colonel Archibald Campbell to Georgia to capture Savannah. That city was eventually captured on 29 December 1778 when a second British contingent arrived from Florida. The combined force then set about 'pacifying' the rest of Georgia. The Florida contingent, commanded by Major General Prevost, conducted a series of raids along the coast. It was not until the spring of 1779 that Washington could send a detachment of Continental regulars under General Benjamin Lincoln to the area. Lincoln's initial objective, the recapture of Augusta, failed.

In June 1779 Spain declared war on England and began taking an active role in supplying the Americans with war materiels. In September a French naval force of approximately 6000 men and 35 warships arrived off Savannah. Combining their efforts with Lincoln's 1400 troops they laid siege to the city. The French commander Comte d'Estaing was too impatient to maintain the siege and, after ordering a full assault on the fortress on 9 October, he gave up the effort and sailed to the West Indies, returning Lincoln's regulars to the city of Charleston.

With the failure of the efforts to recapture Augusta and Savannah Clinton was encouraged to believe that a series of rapid successful engagements might dishearten the Americans and their French allies and bring the war to a swift conclusion. He moved the majority of his forces south using Savannah as his primary base of operations. He then collected the British garrison from Rhode Island and on 26 December 1779 combined those troops with 8000 from New York and moved at once against his new objective, Charleston, South Carolina. Although the New York garrison was reduced it remained 10,000 strong,

Above: General Lincoln lost Charleston to the British.
Above right: General Cornwallis.
Right: General Berthier, later famous as Napoleon's Chief of Staff, served with Rochambeau.

prohibiting Washington from capitalizing on the change in the British plan and so in December he moved his army to Morristown for the winter.

By the spring of 1780 the southern situation was very strongly in British favor. Clinton entered Charleston harbor in February with little difficulty. The harbor forts had fallen into disrepair and were no problem for Clinton's troops to overcome. Lincoln had made a fatal error by placing his troops directly in the city rather than the surrounding countryside and by early April he was trapped. Unable to break out of Charleston Lincoln acknowledged that the situation was lost and surrendered his army, which had grown to a force of 5000, almost half of whom were Continental regulars. This was the worst defeat suffered by the Americans during the Revolutionary War. In many circles the phrase 'beginning of the end' became widely used. Clinton returned to New York, satisfied that South Carolina would be secured, leaving General Cornwallis in command of 8000 men.

In the north the Continental Army was suffering other equally serious problems. In May Washington was faced with mutiny by two Connecticut regiments which he was finally forced to disarm. Although no one was injured in that demonstration against lack of pay and deplorable conditions it was a clear indication that something had to be done soon to improve the situation of the army. Politics were playing an unappreciated role in events. Washington became increasingly opposed to the mandates and dictates of the Continental Congress and he accused its members of being more involved in their own power struggles than in the army or the cause. After the mutiny Washington pardoned all troops who participated, as a gesture of good faith and to demonstrate that he understood their problems.

Also in May a British-Tory force under Tory leader Lieutenant Colonel Banastre Tarleton massacred a Patriot contingent of 300 at a place known as Waxhaw Creek. As though the various events of the war were not sufficiently troublesome Washington again clashed with the Continental Congress over his appointment of Baron Kalb to command 1000 troops in South Carolina. The Congress had also appointed General Gates commander of the south ordering him to gain control over the situation and contain Cornwallis. The Continental Congress knew Washington had specifically requested that General Nathaniel Greene be given that role but Greene was not a popular figure and Gates continued to exert strong political influence in the Congress. While the debate raged a French army of 5000 men commanded by Comte de Rochambeau with a full naval escort landed at Newport, Rhode Island. Washington hoped that with the addition of this French force he could wrest New York away from Clinton. His hopes were destroyed when a British fleet blockaded Newport trapping the French.

Attention focussed on the south as Gates arrived in South Carolina in July 1780. His army was more than 4000 strong, with at least 2000 Continental regulars provided by Washington. Gates decided to begin his campaign by marching on the British supply depot at Camden, South Carolina. However, on the morning of 16 August Cornwallis caught Gates completely by surprise north of that town. After a series of blunders by their commander Gates' army lost heart and fled. In the rout, known as the 'Camden Race' the American troops threw down their weapons and scattered into the countryside. The British force, which was only half the size of Gates', took full advantage of the unprecedented rout. When the engagement was over 2000 Americans were killed, wounded or captured. Baron Kalb was among the dead. Repercussions from the defeat ran through the colonies. Washington found the support he needed to have Gates removed and Greene established as the commander of operations in the south but the defeat meant that the

largest and best-organized American force there had been destroyed. It also meant that there was nothing to block Cornwallis' advance into North Carolina.

Cornwallis began his offensive against North Carolina in October. He decided to approach the invasion with three separate forces. He himself would retain command of the main army, comprised entirely of British and Hessian regulars. Lieutenant Colonel Tarleton was placed in command of a Legion of Tory cavalry and light infantry and the third force of 1100 Tory troops was commanded by Major Patrick Ferguson. Both Tarleton and Ferguson commanded some of the best Tory units in the British service. Ferguson particularly had spent a great deal of time on drill and discipline and his troops were virtually on a par with any British regiment. Moreover Ferguson was in addition a proponent of advancements in infantry weapons. His most important contribution to this aspect of warfare was his development of the Ferguson Rifle. This weapon was the first successful breech-loading infantry weapon. Its rapid reload capability resulted from a mechanism which enabled the user to turn the base of the trigger guard and open the breech to provide a space at the top of the barrel into which ball and powder could be placed. The rifle gave soldiers a rate of fire three or four times faster than muzzle-loaded weapons. Although the weapons did not have the range of the Pennsylvania or Kentucky Long Rifle it was comparable to any

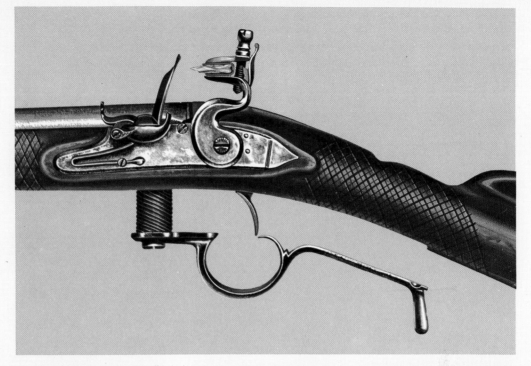

British weapon or the Hessian Jaeger Rifle. Had Ferguson survived the Carolina campaign and promoted his invention the entire face of warfare might have been changed by the widespread introduction of a breech-loading weapon to the world's battlefields.

Ferguson's and Tarleton's combined mission was to eliminate any American resistance in western South Carolina while Cornwallis continued his advance north. Tarleton was assigned to the westernmost flank of the campaign which was known to be an area sympathetic to the Revolution. As Ferguson's force moved into the Appalachian Mountain area a call to arms was given to the mountain men of Scottish and Irish descent. This Patriot force was commanded by Isaac Shelby. The opposing forces met on 7 October 1780 at King's Mountain on the border between North and South Carolina. Ferguson had established his camp on top of the mountain, which leveled out to a large rolling plateau 60 feet above the surrounding countryside. The plateau was approximately 600 yards long and 250 yards wide. The Patriot force which advanced on the mountain consisted of ten units of 50–200 men each. Many of the men were familiar with the recent massacre perpetrated by Tarleton's troops and were anxious to seek revenge. As Ferguson waited for a break in the weather the frontiersmen surrounded the plateau. Shelby's intended tactics were simple. The Patriot troops nearest the Tory camp were to open fire and drive the Tories down the neck of the plateau where waiting Patriots would ambush them.

The battle opened with a volley of fire then a charge on the Tory camp. Ferguson reacted immediately, rallying his troops from their bivouac by the use of a whistle. He had trained his men to respond to its blast as they would to bugle or drum. Nonetheless the Tory troops were caught off guard and although they attempted to defend they were forced to fall back. As Ferguson struggled to rally his men one of his officers raised a white flag but Ferguson charged his horse at it and cut it down. He then ordered his men to attempt to break away. The frontiersmen had drawn close to the Tory position and recognizing Ferguson as the commander of the force directed their fire at him. Both Ferguson and his horse were killed instantly. With his death the Tory units collapsed. It then took all Shelby's energies to keep the frontiersmen from murdering their captives.

The victory at King's Mountain heralded the

ultimate defeat of the British campaign in the south and broke the Tory stranglehold in the area. In December Greene arrived in Charlotte, North Carolina. He immediately proceeded to divide his army into small units for quick, effective raids against Cornwallis' forces and other areas of British control. Greene had neither the men nor the materiel to challenge Cornwallis in a set battle but his raiding tactics would be extremely effective. He sent a force under General Daniel Morgan toward Cowpens. A slightly larger force which he kept under his own personal command advanced toward Cheraw. On 17 January 1781 Tarleton's force advancing from Winnesborough engaged Morgan at Cowpens. The attack began at 0645 hours and was immediately met by Morgan's riflemen, who had been placed in skirmish order ahead of his main force. Tarleton continued to advance and when the skirmishers withdrew he charged, confident that he would crush the American defenders. His advance was halted by the staunch defense of Continental troops. Tarleton, remaining confident, sent units of the 71st Highlanders under the command of Major McArthur, to the left to outflank Morgan's line. Morgan's situation was critical but as the Highlanders advanced he played his trump. On command Colonel William Washington's Continental Cavalry charged Tarleton's right flank and a contingent of mounted militia struck the left while the riflemen returned to the line to bolster Morgan's center. The envelopment of both flanks and increased fire from the center threw Tarleton's force into chaos. He tried desperately to rally his men but when Tarleton and his cavalry were engaged by Colonel Washington's cavalry his force broke and routed from the field. Later reports stated that Tarleton fled chased by Washington himself.

Two months later the American forces struck the final blow against Cornwallis, who had continued his advance into North Carolina. Although Cornwallis pursued Morgan's force, the American units eluded the British and reunited with Greene. Greene, with a reinforced army of more than 4000 decided that he was now in a position to meet Cornwallis. On 15 March the armies engaged at Guilford Courthouse in one of the most desperate battles of the southern campaign. The Americans, drawn up in three lines, had almost taken the day when Cornwallis brought his reserve artillery on to the battlefield. Although his own troops were locked in hand-to-hand combat with the Americans Cornwallis ordered his artillery to fire on the American lines. Greene was forced to withdraw. Cornwallis claimed victory at the Battle of Guilford Courthouse but it was a hollow triumph in light of his 25 percent casualty rate.

Guilford Courthouse marked the end of Cornwallis' offensive. The defeats of Ferguson and Tarleton and the duration of the campaign had weakened his army to the point where it could no longer be considered

Above: French guns bombard the British defenses at Yorktown.

effective. He retreated to Wilmington, North Carolina. Once there he decided that the Carolinas could never be pacified and through April and May 1781 he moved his army to Virginia. Although Greene could not claim battle victories he had broken the British southern campaign, driving them from the area until only Charleston, South Carolina, remained under British control. Greene remained in the Carolinas to secure that area, leaving the ultimate destruction of Cornwallis to Washington.

After his arrival in Virginia Cornwallis joined forces with Benedict Arnold, who had been given a British commission, and General Phillips which brought his army to a strength of 7000 men. The American force in the area, under the command of General von Steuben, was overwhelmingly outnumbered and could do little to curb Cornwallis' destructive raids. Washington then sent the Marquis de Lafayette with three Continental regiments in support of von Steuben. With Lafayette's arrival Cornwallis moved his base of operations to the coast. By 4 August his army was at Yorktown under the watchful eyes of Lafayette and von Steuben. The situation was definitely weighted in the Americans' favor. The French general Rochambeau marched his army from Rhode Island and rendezvoused with Washington. The French fleet had broken from the British blockade and sailed for Virginia to support Washington's impending offensive.

After convincing Clinton that he intended to attack New York City Washington secretly moved his army to Virginia. By the end of August the French fleet had reinforced Lafayette with more than 3000 men and then enforced a blockade of Chesapeake Bay. On 5 September Admiral Graves attempted to break the blockade but was defeated and forced to return to New York. When the British fleet abandoned him Cornwallis realized that he had no alternative but to fortify the entire area if he was to have any hope of saving his position. His initial plans called for a double line of fortifications to be constructed around Yorktown. His assembled force included men from the Royal Navy, a contingent of Guards, seven regiments of British infantry and a number of Hessian and Loyalists units who all set to work immediately on those defenses. Cornwallis also established a fortification across the York River at Gloucester where he placed a garrison of 700 men. In support of his defenses he had 65 artillery pieces. Cornwallis hoped he would have time to prepare an adequate defense and provisions for the winter.

Although the British completed three redoubts Washington struck before the defensive perimeter was established. On 14 September Washington appeared with 6000 Continental regulars, which he added to the 3000 Virginia militia and Rochambeau's 8000 men. He had Cornwallis outnumbered more than two to one. Throughout September the American army grew as more volunteers joined the ranks. Cornwallis realized that he could not possibly defend the perimeter and consolidated his forces on the inner line around the city itself. Although a state of siege existed, formal siege was not laid until 9 October when American and French artillery began to bombard the Yorktown defenses. Washington fired the first shot himself and almost immediately the earthworks Cornwallis had constructed began to crumble. General Thomas Nelson, Governor of Virginia and commander of the local militia, encouraged the artillerymen by aiming a cannon directly at his stately Yorktown home. In so doing he demonstrated his support for the unpleasant task of bombarding the city while at the same time striking a blow at Cornwallis, whom Nelson was certain was using his home as a headquarters. As the artillery fired from positions 500 yards from the British defenses Tarleton clashed with French cavalry on the outskirts of Gloucester. The Tory cavalry force was swiftly defeated but Tarleton escaped by retreating behind formed British regulars who had moved forward to counter the French. By the end of that first day French and American artillery had not only destroyed the earthworks but had also set on fire the 44-gun British warship HMS *Charon* and three transport vessels.

The following day Cornwallis received a message from Clinton assuring him that the New York army was preparing to march to his aid. During the next 48 hours the French and American troops dug a parallel line 300 yards from the British inner defense. On 14 October two assaults, one French and one American captured two of the British redoubts. Although the British counterattacked to stabilize the situation Cornwallis' position had become critical. Fewer than 3000 of his army were fit for action. With insufficient troops to break the siege or defend against a concerted assault Cornwallis decided to attempt to evacuate the city by crossing with his troops to Gloucester. On the night of 16 October Cornwallis implemented his evacuation plans despite a severe storm which hampered his attempts. He soon discovered that Washington had second guessed him and had reinforced the Gloucester Peninsula. Cornwallis could do no more. On the morning of 17 October he asked Washington upon what terms he would accept surrender. On 18 October, in bright new uniforms, Cornwallis' army laid down their arms, marching to the music 'The World Turned Upside-Down.' Cornwallis assigned the official surrender to his second in command Major General Charles O'Hara as the illness he had been suffering overcame him. O'Hara surrendered his sword to General Benjamin Lincoln. Ironically on 19 October Clinton sailed with a relief force of more than 7000 men. On the Virginia coast his fleet rescued a small boat containing three men who had escaped from Yorktown. When their story was told Clinton turned back to New York. The southern campaign sealed the fate of the British armies, assuring victory for the Revolution.

9 A NEW NATION

When the news of the state of affairs in the Americas reached Parliament in early 1782 the advocates of peace were finally heard and negotiations with the Continental Congress begun. The war would continue until 1783 but no further battles of major importance occurred. In April 1782 official discussions began between the Crown and representatives of the 'American Peace Negotiations Committee.' Benjamin Franklin opened the talks, later to be joined by John Adams, Henry Laurens and John Jay. Preliminary outlines were made describing the needs and demands of both Britain and America. Serious negotiations began in September 1782.

The American commissioners secured three principal terms in the treaty. First and most importantly the United States of America was declared fully independent and granted all the rights and privileges of a sovereign nation. Second, Britain

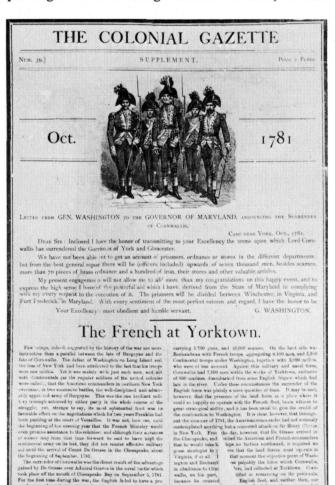

relinquished all claim to land between the Appalachian Mountains and the Mississippi and those territories from the Great Lakes in the north to Florida in the south. Florida, which had been acquired by Britain in 1763, was returned to Spain, a change which would cause friction between Spain and America until 1795. Finally, American fishermen gained the right to fish in the Gulf of St Lawrence and along the coast of Newfoundland. Stalemates in the negotiations came over the issues of debts and property. The Tory element in the States believed that their loyal support of the Crown was worth recompense and demanded that Parliament force the Continental Congress to return all properties and lands confiscated during the war. This was impossible as most of the properties involved had been sold years earlier to finance the war and the Continental Congress had no funds with which they could compensate the Tories, which the Congress would not have been inclined to do in any case. These questions concerning war debts and compensation were finally answered by a compromise proposal. Britain and the United States agreed to recommend that claimants against the Continental Congress take their cases before the courts in America. This compromise was a token gesture on the part of the Congress as it had no intention of forcing the courts to hear cases of Tory or British claims. The Tory population realized these basic facts and most of them took the possessions they had left and moved to Canada.

The preliminary agreement was signed in November 1782 and ratified by the Continental Congress in April 1783. The final peace treaty was signed in Paris on 3 September 1783. It was not until December of that year that the last British troops, commanded by Clinton, sailed from New York harbor. France accused Britain of 'buying' peace but Great Britain had been at war too long and its relations with nations around the world were strained. As one Member of Parliament allegedly replied, 'If this is buying peace then it is cheap at any cost.'

What had the American Revolution accomplished? Obviously a new nation was created and 13 individual colonies were bound under one government. The idealists, men like Thomas Jefferson, envisioned the revolution as a means of achieving and securing

personal freedom. The realists, such as Samuel Adams and John Hancock, achieved the economic climate they had sought, securing their investments and those of men like them by the land and fishing terms of the peace treaty. They had eliminated Britain's restrictive hand and were now prepared to use their influence to set the country on a course of their choosing.

This was the harsh reality behind the revolution, yet the American War of Independence assumes a far more meaningful position in the history of man. Although the Continental Congress betrayed many of those who fought for independence, giving worthless vouchers in lieu of promised bonuses and confiscating and selling their properties for back taxes levied by the States, the ideal would live on. The colonists were rugged individualists. They had carved a prosperous nation from a hostile wilderness and they would do so again. Their journals, diaries and letters demonstrate the vision they possessed. The embodiment of their ideals, The Declaration of Independence, is perhaps the most perfect document ever composed. The concept of a nation 'conceived in liberty' and 'dedicated to justice for all' is a cause for which the American people have continued to commit the ultimate sacrifice.

Above: The ragged troops of the Continental Army march into New York at the end of the war.
Far left: The *Colonial Gazette* announces Cornwallis' surrender.
Below: The last British troops leave New York.

INDEX

Page references in italics refer to illustrations.

Acknowledgements

The author would like to thank Adrian Hodgkins who designed this book and Penny Murphy who compiled the index. The following agencies and individuals kindly supplied the illustrations.

Bison Picture Library: 19 top, 26–27, 34, 46, 59 top, 62
Library of Congress: 7, 9 bottom, 14, 17, 22, 29, 39, 48 bottom, 49 right, 52 top right
Robert Hunt Picture Library: 58
Mansell Collection: 23
Samuel L Morison Collection: 56
National Archives (US): 6, 13 top, 31
National Army Museum (UK): 18, 47 right, 48 top, 49 left, 57 bottom right
New York Public Library (via Robert Hunt): 1
Peter Newark's Western Americana: 2–3, 9 top, 10, 11, 12, 13 bottom, 16, 21 all three, 28, 33 top, 35 both, 36 both, 37, 38, 40–41, all three, 42 both, 43, 44–45 all three, 47 left, 53 bottom, 57 top left, 59 bottom, 60–61, 63 bottom
US Army: 18–19, 51 bottom
US Navy: 4–5, 25, 30–31, 33 bottom, 52, 53 top, 54, 55 both.